My Uphill Battle

MARVIN EDGARDO ORTIZ

Copyright © 2017 Marvin Edgardo Ortiz

All rights reserved.

ISBN: 1547030828
ISBN-13: 978-1547030828

DEDICATION

This is for the most important ladies in my life, my mother Rosa Ortiz and my wife Gabriela Ortiz who have always been there for me, and to all my Mexican friends who I owe my deepest gratitude for taking this journey along with me. A special thanks to Blanca Morales who has been like a guardian angel to me.

CONTENTS

1	Chapter: A unique childhood in Los Angeles	Pg.1
2	Chapter: School's dead dogmas and where it led me	Pg.7
3	Chapter: A mother's effort sometimes is not enough	Pg.15
4	Chapter: The metamorphosis that turned me into a madman	Pg.19
5	Chapter: The beginning of my punishments, first deportation to El Salvador	Pg.25
6	Chapter: United States of Corporate America and modern day slavery	Pg.35
7	Chapter: Second deportation to El Salvador	Pg.41
8	Chapter: Salvadoran gangs and the misconceptions	Pg.45
9	Chapter: Always better to carry a gun and not need it, than to need one and not have it	Pg.49
10	Chapter: Results of extreme culture shock	Pg.55

11	Chapter: An animal's eyes have the power to comfort	Pg.59
12	Chapter: The first job ever in my life	Pg.61
13	Chapter: El Salvador, the murder capital of the world	Pg.65
14	Chapter: Tendentious laws are result for incompetence	Pg.69
15	Chapter: Problems at the Guatemalan border	Pg.81
16	Chapter: Failure in Costa Rica	Pg.83
17	Chapter: Homies or humbugs, they are all over the world	Pg.87
18	Chapter: Back in Guatemala with a new plan	Pg.91
19	Chapter: At the Mexican border of Talisman	Pg.101
20	Chapter: Immigration institution and its corruption	Pg.113
21	Chapter: In the quest for Cujo	Pg.113
22	Chapter: The strife has come to an end	Pg.121

CHAPTER 1
A UNIQUE CHILDHOOD IN LOS ANGELES

My real name is Marvin, but most people in the streets of South L.A and in prison know me as *Smiley*. That's the moniker I was given during my youth. We all had monikers in the city where I grew up. That's how things work in Los Angeles.

My childhood years were spent in California, the inner city of South Central Los Angeles, to be exact. I lived in an overcrowded house with my mother, my grandmother, an uncle, an aunt, four cousins, three brothers and me. It was the typical Mexican home only that we were not Mexican. My family migrated from El Salvador in the beginning of 1978. I was only fifteen months young when I was brought to the United States of America. Out of all my brothers and cousins, I was the only one born there. The rest were born in the United States, lucky for them. They did not have to go through the struggle I had to go through; quite frankly, I do not thing none would have survived.

I never met my father, and never felt the desire to

have known him. He denied me when I was born. In any case it's only good to know a father when he is a good father. Otherwise is best not to even know his name. My point is, screw him.

My family was indigent, we were products of welfare but I never knew that at the time. Outside of the house I had more cousins, aunts and uncles. At one point they all meant something to me. We were a huge family. My huge family would celebrate holidays like Christmas and Thanksgiving together, and always at my house because that was where grandma lived. And she was the head of the family after all. During the holiday celebrations, my grandma liked to gather around the table and play poker with my uncles and aunts. She would always win because she would be the only sober one at the table while everyone else got drunk. She enjoyed taking their money, and my uncles and aunts enjoyed seeing grandma happy. She thought of herself as the best poker player in the family.

My uncles and aunts used to send us, children to fetch them more beer each time they wanted another while they went on with their poker game. I would open the can for them and take a drink when they were not looking before handing the beer over. When they were drunk enough, my cousins and I would steal the beer from the fridge and have our own party mimicking them in a poker table of our own. They were too drunk to notice the missing beer cans.

During the poker game they would sit around and lay money on the table, and yes, we would steal that as well. We did not steal huge amounts of money, just small change something for the sweet tooth.

My family aided one another in the times of need. We were so close, it was a wonderful family. However, time dismantles families, and boy does it tear them apart. As time passes by we simply become relatives sometimes even enemies. But despite of what I've gone through, I would not change that childhood for the world. Through it I've attained valuable lessons it made me the man I am today. You should never be afraid to go through a struggle. If we allow it, pain transforms us to something better. Sometimes you just have to let life teach you a good lesson and not take it personal.

The city of Los Angeles is not all glamour like they make it appear in T.V. Los Angeles is the gang capital of America. So guess what, if you are living in Los Angeles it is more than likely you will become a gang member. There are over one thousand gangs and over one-hundred-thousand gang members in Los Angeles County alone. The vast majority of the population where I grew up was Blacks and Mexicans; there were no white families that I can remember.

Drugs were sold everywhere during the time that I lived there, and things have not changed much since, drugs are still being sold, immensely. Many people in the neighborhood sold them. My neighbors sold them in the corner while they shot dice and drank *40oz. Old English*. They were Crips. Most of them were my school friends' relatives. They would call themselves by names like *Eazy-Bone*, *C-Rag*, and *Nutty* which I found very funny as a child. When I used to walk by them, they would say: *"wassup Little Man."* I'd return the greeting by nodding my head and saying *"wassup"* in return. They called me *Little Man* because of my height obviously. I've always been quite small in height. When I was seven-years old, I appeared to be five. When I was ten-years old, I appeared to be seven. I never grew much. I'm not sure why, but I suppose that my height is just a side effect that comes with premature children.

Drive-by shootings were common in the area, almost nightly I'd be awakening by the sound of gun fire and sirens. During the afternoons there were also shootings.

One day while my neighbors were shooting dice and drinking their *40oz. Old English*, a vehicle from a rival gang drove by. Shots were fired from the vehicle. The shots came from a twelve gauge shotgun. The shooter had turned my way, we made eye contact and for a split second I thought he was going to shoot me as well, but he did not. After the car fled away, I ran to the street to pick up the shotgun shells that were left on the street. I'm not sure why I did that, curiosity I guess. I was nine-years-old at the time.

A half hour later LAPD arrived to the scene. They went door to door asking the neighbors including us if we had seen or heard anything regarding the shooting. I had seen it all, but told them that I did not see anything. I still had the shotgun shells in my pocket, and kept them as a relic of what I had seen. That was the second shooting that I had experienced at close range at a very young age.

In spite of the perils around me, I never felt threaten by the people I was surrounded by. Gang members did not make my neighborhood unsafe. I actually felt more threaten by the LAPD. Just seeing the look in their pale faces filled with malice made me insecure and made me tremble as a child. That fear turned into hatred towards them as I grew older. They never brought anything good to the neighborhood. They patrol to victimize under their crappy slogan; *"Protect and Serve."* Each time they came around the neighborhood it was to slander, provoke, and threat the community. They treated us like criminals even before we were criminals. I have homeboys that are spending the rest of their lives in prison because they were frame by these crooked bastards. I had seen them beat and shoot teens just because they could and get away with it. Their way of performing their job gave me ample reason to mistrust them from day one. I despised seeing them around the neighborhood.

Police officers have a way to make children feel inferior and somehow undeserving of anything better in life. By the time I became a teen I felt like the pathology of a healthy society; as a marginal who has strayed from the general provisions of a "good, organized, and just" society. From my point of view their goal is to turn everyone into a criminal, and the truth is they are the real criminals.

Inner cities have always been dealing with police terrorism. In recent years their terrorism has spread to the suburbs and different parts of American. It's happening everywhere now. Even White Americans are getting a taste of what inner cities have been dealing with for decades. America is becoming a police state from the looks of it and very few are noticing.

MARVIN E. ORTIZ

CHAPTER 2
SCHOOL'S DEAD DOGMA AND WHERE IT LED ME

Every morning before class, we would pledge allegiance to the American flag. The only flag I've ever pledged my allegiance to. For a long time I had the habit of placing my left hand over my chest during the pledge. The teacher would correct me each time by saying; *"use your other right hand."* I suppose this could be a habit with most left-handed kids.

Throughout elementary I received countless awards, and I was always an honor roll student. I had inspired to really become someone in life. Learning came easy for me.

I attended a total of three different elementary schools throughout my life: *49th street, 107th street,* and *Hyde Park* all in the ghetto of Los Angeles. The first shooting I had experienced was in elementary when I was eight-years-old. It happened February 24, 1984 in *49th Street Elementary School*. The gunman was a 28-year-old individual by the name of Tyrone Mitchell. He was armed with an AR-15, Stoeger 12 gauge double-barreled shotgun, and a Winchester 12 gauge pump-action shotgun. The shooting took place after school. Upon hearing the rapid shots being fire my instinct was to run in search of my little brother and two cousins.

After school we would always meet in the schoolyard to walk home together, and that's where the shooting took place. The shooting lasted approximately fifteen minutes. A ten-year-old girl by the name of Shala Eubanks had gotten shot. She later died inside a classroom after she was carried there by school staff. There was a total of fourteen people injured, two that died, not including the shooter who committed suicide by shooting himself in the head with the double-barreled shotgun. All of the victims were either Black or Hispanic. I never recall the media making big fuzz about this school shooting. I doubt America recalls it, but I still do.

Everything changed in Jr. High School. I was finding contradictions on the lectures of my teachers. They spoke as if the world was a safe place while I was witnessing otherwise. Their lessons suffered from malpractice and were detached from the reality I was living. From that, my life took a sudden turn and it was all about ridding the bad energies. I did not mean for that to happen, never realizing that my life was heading towards a bad direction, it all came by surprise. Many of the teenagers in *Henry Clay Jr. High School* belonged to a gang, including many of friends.

In Jr. High School is where I first met Ismael Arredondo, my homeboy *Lonely*, and my good friend Blanca Morales. I started deviating from school by first skipping school with my homeboy *Lonely* and going to, what was known as a "ditching party." Ditching parties consisted of, obviously skipping school, heading to a friend's house to consume alcohol, smoke weed, and make-out with girls. Lonely and I were charming, and famous with the girls. We always had the privilege of enjoying the ditching parties with them. I found myself skipping school so much and hanging around with the gang that at the age of twelve-years old, I just decided to drop out of school and I became a gang member. Needless to say I had joined a Mexican gang. After all, school was not teaching me how to survive in the world I was living in as far as I concern. There could have been other factors why I had decided to join a gang for example; the lack of after school programs, the search for a father figure, or the desire to just form part of a social group. Whatever it was, it filled a void.

To join a Mexican gang from Los Angeles it does not require going out and shooting someone down. The only requirement was to take a half a minute beaten by three individuals from the same gang. To me being part of a gang was like being part of a baseball team where we all received a unique name like, *Turtle, Cricket, Hippo, Wicked* or *Lucky*. That's when I first received the pseudo of *Smiley*, though the Crips by my house still called me *Little Man*.

For those who are not familiar with inner cities. In the inner cities we've always used monikers to identify ourselves, and use different jives like the word *"homeboy"* or for short *"homie"* to identify a fellow member. Therefore my peers that formed the social group of South Los Angeles are my homeboys.

In our gatherings we would have parties, drink beer, dance and experiment with drugs. I remember the first time that I smoked PCP, what's also known as *Angel Dust*. I had smoked with my homeboys, *Yankee, Hippo, Lonely* and *Rascal*. It was at a neighborhood party, we were all moving in slow motion but in motion dancing to George Clinton's *Atomic Dog*. I'm glad cellphones did not exist then. The whole world would have seen us dance like fools.

Nothing was ever imposed on me by the gang. There were no obligations, what I did was because I chose to do it. Though I did things that I'm not proud of, and said things I did not mean. A gang teaches you how to hate people that I should not have to hate. Nothing good comes out of joining a gang that I can assure you. It automatically turns you into an enemy of a lot of people; it limits your boundaries, limits your friends, and instills hate in your heart and poignant that manifests with violence. For, violence is extroverted pain. You might want to remember that next time your child lashes out at someone.

I used to live about twenty miles away from 111st and Vermont in Los Angeles, the place where we used to all gather to hang out. That place we called the *"barrio,"* or the "hood." Due to the distance between my house and the hood, often I just spent the nights at my homeboy *Lonely* or homegirl *Beaver's* house. Her mother *Doña* Rogelia was very nice to me. She would always welcome me with her homemade *tamales*, which I liked very much. She even worried when I did not go home with *Beaver*. *Doña* Rogelia used to worry for good reason. Death was eminent to anyone of us during that era.

There was a terrible territorial gang war happening with some Crips that was just a few blocks down. We walked the streets constantly looking over our shoulder expecting for someone to drive by and riddle us with gun fire.

Being part of a gang was not like I had thought at first. It starts as all fun and games with parties, alcohol and women and it ends with watching your peers bleed, scream, or die when there's the option of watching you laugh, live and shine. Some attended graduations while I was attending funerals. By the age of sixteen I had attended more funerals than many will ever attend in two life times. Once I attended two funerals in one day.

During 1991-1992 were some of the worse years that I can remember for South Los Angeles. Many of us were not even making it pass the age of nineteen. Death had teased me countless times, but I was fortunate. Flirting with death and feeling her cold chilling touch was part of the game. Sooner or later my luck would run out I thought, and I'd picture my own funeral. Several times I imagined that. Thus I lived like if there was no tomorrow. The fact of one day being killed is something any gang member has to face and by accepting that, it striped me of all fear.

Society influenced me to take wrong actions, from wrong actions I developed the wrong habits and from the wrong habits, I developed the wrong character; a character that was tailored to survive my environment, in the real world! I held the mask of my character tightly to my face, scare to let go. I was so frighten to let it go that I was willing to die fulfilling my role for an audience striving towards an existence by pleasing the audience with my own displeasing. I think many us did that.

In the isolated world of South Los Angeles we engrave our own history with legends, heroes and martyrs that are known by names like *Cartoon, Trusty, Lil Mono, Lil Moreno, Dreamer, Spider, Greedy;* boys that died like men, brethren that have lost their lives to a cruel society. Their memory forever ingrained in many hearts. And yet, there are other homies buried alive in men-made cells, kept away from their loved ones and forever striped from their freedom. Neither predicament is a good place to be in, but those are the realities of becoming a gang member. Nothing is worth that.

Still sometimes we are tottered to building our own prisons. Remember, that not all prisons require walls, bars, or barbed wire fences; it only requires prisoners, prison guards and for us to remain there. South Los Angeles was my childhood prison where I could not escape from. I could not go anywhere, not even to the neighboring cities.

I remember trying to do that once, when I was sixteen. I drove to the suburbs of Pasadena California with my girlfriend. We were on our way to a movie theatre. I was pulled over by Pasadena PD. They asked me where I was from, I told the officer, Los Angeles. The officer told me he did not want to see me in his city, and asked me to back where I belong. I took those words seriously. I did just that, never again did I went outside of South Los Angeles again. I placed an imaginary wall around this city and created my own prison.

I would have given anything to find a way out of Los Angeles; though my family never made an attempt. As a child I could not understand why we did not just pack our bags and move out of the ghetto. This convinced me even further that indeed it was the place where I belong. I had no idea that society was preparing a crime, and I was doom to commit the act.

As an adult I understood the reason why my family never moved out of the ghetto. Welfare played a vital role on keeping my family ghettoized. Welfare hindered my family's social mobility. Remember that welfare only provides enough funds to pay for an inner city house. Furthermore, welfare told us what to eat and how much to eat through the food stamps. Consequently, it alienated me. My family failed to realize that we were outcast in the inner city of Los Angeles. Welfare is not free; it has a price and a dear one.

Sadly, it often takes the loss of a loved one to awaken us from the crucially of the *status quo*. My family took many lost before realizing what the inner city brought. They know what it means to lose a child to drugs, a prison and death. If you are not ready to take this lost, and I do not think anyone is, break yourself free from the ball of chain of welfare know that there are better opportunities elsewhere.

Welfare is a criminal broth which is ladled out in the country under a deceitful name and we must be very careful on how to use it. You must learn how to play the game of the system. Gang members do not just grow out of the ground like a carrot. We are the fruits of our environment in which we are rooted.

MARVIN E. ORTIZ

SATAN'S GAME

Satan has found Himself a sweet domain

Out on the coast of Southern West,

Where the Brown and Black are put to

---- A deadly quest.

This city is blanketed with thousands of gloomy clouds,

That pours rain and strikes thunder----

On all the

Angels who roam down under.

I; a Brown Angel, you a Black one,

We whom are pressed down, down!

Unto the Beast's fuming fire.

It is there where He rules, where He laughs

Playing His sick dark games of sorrow

The game of death, taking our last breath of air

---- Tomorrow.

CHAPTER 3
A MOTHER'S EFFORT SOMETIMES IS NOT ENOUGH

My mother's effort to guide me on the "right path," as she often would say were futile against a rebellious child caught in the web of the inner city. South Los Angeles was easy – a little too easy – to get into trouble, in which I did. Perhaps things would have been different if the right path had been shown to me through action and conviction, and not just words.

The sternness of a father was missing, and the gentleness of a mother, I had in abundance. My mother was not the kind of woman that took me across the knees to show me a good lesson. She was always patience with me. Too patient I'd say not that a good beaten would have made me understand. I was living in an ambiance that prohibited understanding, and rewarded those who broke the law. Breaking the law was the thing to do. Crime was a rife, and a way of life. I can clearly recall my mother's words; *"son, you're always messing things up,"* or *"can't you do something better with your life?"* I'd always promise my mother that I change. I sought for a "right path" to follow, I really did, but I could not find one. It's a grave mistake to say that I knew better when in fact I was not shown any better.

The right path illusion will always be a tumbling rock in the way of parent thought. Indeed, at the end it was my choice to choose from the paths that were there for me, and I chose. One month after my seventeenth birthday (August of 1993), I chose to rob a *Mc Donald's* restaurant. I held it at gun point using a Tech-nine or the "evil gun" has is best known in the streets. My girlfriend at the time was close to giving birth to my twin daughters: Angel and Priscilla Ortiz. I wanted the money to provide for them. That was my motive for that robbery. I wanted to give them everything I could. It never crossed my mind to work instead. For, that was never shown to me.

At the end I was not there during my daughters' birth. On September 29, 1993 I was in jail detained for arm robbery. My daughters are now twenty-three years old and I still have not been there for them. Fortunately, they were blessed to have the father figure in their lives that did a hell of a job on raising them. I completely failed them. Was that robbery worth it? Of course it was not.

At the time of my arrest, authorities were already looking for me. I had shot two individuals two months prior. The shooting was not gang related. The shooting took place over a family dispute. The conflict was not even with me.

Most families have a black sheep in the family. The black sheep is often bashed or tongue lash by his own family members. Often he's looked at as a disgrace to the family, as a low life. In the times of your most desperate need, no one in the family will come to succor you but the black sheep. You can always count on him to do whatever it takes in order to help the situation. We all need a black sheep in the family, and we need to treat him right.

Unfortunately for the individuals who chose to

conflict with my family. I happened to be the black sheep of mine family, violence was my way of reasoning. As a result to this conflict, I shot a man five times in the chest with a .380 caliber pistol. He stayed in a coma for forty days and his nephew I shot once in the leg. I never asked my family member what the dispute was about, or who was at fault. I really did not care. I just acted to protect my family. I paid dearly for what I did. My actions led me to prison for a long time. Though, I think life in South Los Angeles can justify far worse crimes than the ones attributed to me. Nonetheless, I am grateful for the time that I spent in prison. It opened my eyes to many things in life, and awoke a conscious I did not know I had.

Little that I knew that prison was not going to be the only punishment I was going to receive for the things that I had committed. The real punishments came after I was release from prison.

In L.A County jail I met inmates that were facing execution. Some are awaited execution now, all because they too failed to follow another man's path. Right from wrong has to be taught with conviction. The death penalty can be imposed and it will be of no use. To sentence a man to die on the electric chair (*old sparky*) for failing to follow a right path, is not to convince him that there was an alternative. The volts from the electric chair are flickered, yet it does not seem intrinsic to the dying man's issue. He does not doubt that the volts are going to electrocute him; but perchance his frying mind may recollect all the paths he ever knew when he was a child as he dies in his belief that he opted what seemed right to him, and never would he get to know the *"right path."*

MARVIN E. ORTIZ

MY DAUGHTERS' BIRTHDAY

Today is you two special day,
I think of you both,
For there is nothing I could say.

My mind wonders woeful and weary
With some questions to me that are dreary.
Did you get the dress you so desired?

Did you dance and laugh?
And was everything well prepared and gathered?
Have you even thought of me? ----
Your foreign father?

I'm in the blink of going into a fray,
I want to throw my fists unto the cells walls,
Do all I can to release my wrath,
By breaking everything along my path.
Instead, I sit till the night is gone,
Hoping you two were placed on a
Princesses' thrones.

CHAPTER 4
THE METAMORPHOSIS THAT TURNED ME INTO A MADMAN

It took almost two years before I was found guilty of all counts: attempt to murder, assault with a deadly weapon, and two counts of arm robbery. I received a total of twenty-two years. The judge said he was lenient on me because I was underage at the time of my arrest.

Through the course of my prison sentence I was transfer to many Correctional facilities, but there was one prison that had a great impact on me, and transforms me unto something else. This prison was Corcoran. Corcoran was infamous for its brutality in the late 1980s through the mid-1990s. I arrived at Corcoran in 1995 when things were not as bad as the years before, but the place still gave goose bumps. That prison was not made for just any inmate; no, only the toughest of the toughest walked that prison.

During my time there, I witnessed its gruesomeness. There were a lot of blood-thirsty inmates housed there that wanted to make a name for them. Corcoran at one point was the deadliest prison in American.

In any prison you have to be reciprocal. You either answer with the utmost respect or answer with the utmost brutality that you can. That's just the way it is. A year after my arrival, I was tempered to respond with violence obliged to react by stabbing another inmate. Upon my reaction I was removed from the general population (GP), and placed in the special housing unit, better known as the SHU.

The SHU was what really made Corcoran infamous. Corcoran state prison was also known as the gladiator school with the SHU yard being the battle field. Hispanic and Black inmates were forced into gladiators fights under the barrel of a 37mm better known in prison as "big bertha" and under the barrel of a deadly H&K 9mm. Correctional officers placed bets on set-up fights they arranged. They would choose the healthiest, strongest and biggest Hispanic and Black inmate to fight one another. There were a lot of injured inmates; fortunately there were some that lost their lives murdered by the correctional officer's H&K 9mm shooting.

This came to an end when former correctional officer Richard Caruso and Lt. Steve Rigg decided to break the code of silence and exposed what was happening to the FBI. The former officers provided evidence of the fights and shootings. Caruso and Rigg were forced to retire after their fellow officers had marked them as "rats" and made the working environment impossible for them. Caruso sued the state of California. Eventually the state settled for $1.7 million. The story was cover by *60 Minutes*. The policies in the SHU changed thereafter.

Correctional officers are pretty much the same as LAPD officers. They both induce violence between Hispanics and Blacks. The sad part about this is that we, the minority go along with their games pretending to hate each other for no good reason.

In case you are wondering if I ever participated in one of these Corcoran SHU battles, I did not. At five feet three inches with a weight of one hundred and twenty pounds, I was not an ideal gladiator fighter to anyone.

Although there were other SHU inmates along the tier, I was unable to carry out a conversation with any of the other SHU inmates. Making noise over the tier was against inmate rules. Occasionally people spoke from cell to cell by first apologizing to everyone over the tier for doing so. This was done only when an important message needed to be passing on. Otherwise it was a sign of disrespect to everyone housed there.

Alone in my SHU cell, and without someone to speak with, nightly I'd lie on my concrete bed and thought about my life. I went to sleep thinking about it. There was plenty of time to rewind my entire life events and play it all back. I did this several times attempting to find out where everything had gone wrong.

A correctional officer wheeled a book cart weekly up and down the tiers giving each SHU inmate the option to choose two books from the cart. The first month I declined each time they came by. I had no interest on reading. Instead, I exercised all day and kept myself entertained with some occasional visitor; little critters that made their way into my cell. But then after the first month I grew tired of just exercising for countless hours and talking to critters that did not talk back. Hence, I reluctantly choose two books one day. It took me more than a month to complete them reading just a few pages at a time. The next two books I chose took me a few weeks to read. Subsequently, I became an avid reader devouring any book that I was able to get my hands on at that time.

The books took me to different parts of the world. Never had I realized how vast the world is. It gave me a perspective of life and I started to see life differently. From the solitude of this cell one cold night, my inner flame that I had as a child ignited once again, and it became a consuming inferno turned outwards that I kindled as best as I could.

However, there was something puzzling happening to me. I started hearing an unfamiliar voice coming from inside of my head, another demon I thought; but no, this time it was no demon, it was an articulate voice with a rational discourse that spoke in parallels. I could not understand the content of that voice. Was I becoming mad? More than likely I was. I even felt different. I was no longer discontent with my other self. For the first time in my life I was feeling the presence of my subconscious. And it taunted me day and night.

When I was release back to the general population, people told me that I was not the same anymore. The SHU had made me crazy. The truth is that the time I spent there helped me discover my true identity. I thought differently. I had stopped thinking in plural, in the form of *us* and began to think in the form of *I*: I choose to see things for what they are, not by what others say it is, I choose to speak what's right, not what others, want to hear, I choose to listen to my inner voice, not to foreign verbosity of professional babblers, I choose to lead, and not to be led into disaster.

In general population I continued to read. Books were my ornaments and reading my pastime. The more I read, the better I felt about myself.

Many inmates go through a similar painful metamorphosis, but do not like to show it. Why? Well because we cease to exist within our prison circle. My existence consisted of me being alike the next person, a mirror reflecting another being, of dressing the same, speaking the same, thinking the same, even hating the same way. I had managed to shatter that mirror. To many of my peers I appeared to be a distorted figure; therefore, many of them kept their distance from me. What others were seeing in me was what lay behind the mirror. My peers were no longer seeing their reflection on me. They saw things that were not pleasant, things they could not understand, or things they disliked.

I was also experiencing strange dreams. One in particular I cannot forget. In my dream I had awaken at the same time I always did, and as I reached for the mask that I was going to wear that day I noticed that it was gone. A thief had stolen it, I thought. I became very upset, and desperate without it. I felt sorry for the bastard that had the audacity of stealing from me. I took the sharpest, biggest knife that I had in my cell and ran to the prison yard in search for the thief; though, something else occurred to me that day something unexplainable.

When I stepped out into the yard, I felt the warm sun hit the bare flesh on my face for the very first time. The sun blinded my eyes for a split second, but thereupon all of the anger and hatred that I was carrying inside of me went away. I saw everyone in the prison yard wearing the same mask; using the same jargon, wearing the same style in clothes, enjoying each other's narcissistic company. And that made me sad. In my dream, I was thankful the mask was stolen. Instead of wanting to kill the thief I wanted to embrace him and thank him for taken that mask. I have not been the same person since. From that moment on everyone has said that I lost my mind. That dream was becoming my reality.

After ten years, it was almost time for me to return to the free world. I rewind the life that I lived in South Los Angeles once again. Played it all back one last time to see where I had failed. However, I realized that there was very little that I could have done.

MY CONSCIOUS

There is a humble spirit in my midst,

Entrapped in my morbid body,

In which at first glance---

It may seem as a nobody.

I dare not speak of this spirit's thirst,

Yet here in now----

I do profess, since I'm possess by this spirit

That daunts my chest:

Tide! This mortal in rustic chains

Where it takes away all pain,

Let his blood drip in vain,

For there is nothing more to gain.

Slash him, lash him---- castigate him!

For all his sins.

He was born to suffer, yet imposed

And nothing! Breaks him anymore.

Farewell all his sorrows

From the life he did not borrow.

Once a demon who rode the streets

----To harrow.

Spiritless! With a head filled with pumpkin seeds

Like that of sleepy hallow.

CHAPTER 5
THE BEGINNING OF MY PUNISHMENTS, FIRST DEPORTATION TO EL SALVADOR

It was now the middle of 2003, and time for me to be release. I received a surprise visit from two Immigration Customs Enforcement agents. I was never expecting a visit from them. They had come to pick me up in the day of my release. I was taken to an immigration institution in El Centro California. I went through a court process that lasted two months. It turns out that I was only a *Permanent Resident* of the United States.

The immigration judge told me he was going to send me "home." The only home I knew was in Los Angeles. But that was not where the judge was referring to when he said "home." The judge ordered me removed from the United States. He ordered me to be sent to El Salvador, or "home" as he had put it. I could not believe I was going to be sent to a country I only knew folktales about, but I was. That's the way life is, there's no one else to blame for this but myself.

It did not matter if I had learned how to walk and

speak my first words in the United States. It did not matter if school never taught me how to read or write in Spanish, or if the only allegiance I had pledged was to the United States flag. None of that mattered. Everything that I had ever learned was a farce. I'm sure if the judge would have used a system that was able to compute my whole essence, it would have read: He's American! Yet there's no such system. Even if it was, it would have been inadmissible to the law of the United States which weighs more than the morals of the people.

After a month of being ordered out of the United States the Salvadoran consulate arrived to the detention I was being held at. He called for all Salvadorans awaiting deportation to go see him. His job was to verify their nationality and approve the deportation. When he got to me, he asked where I was born. My mother had told me that I was born in the province of *Santa Ana*. He asked when the dates of the holidays of Santa Ana were, I did not know. He asked to name a typical dish of Santa Ana, I did not know. He asked for the address where I used to live before I left El Salvador, I did not know. He asked me for the address where I was going to live when I got to El Salvador, I did not know. Things did not stop there. The questions went on, and so did the *"I did not knows."*

Throughout the questions and answer process, I noticed he kept looking at me strangely. He finally spoke what he was thinking. He said to me, *"You aren't from El Salvador are you?"* I told him I was born there. He stated something that I was so used of hearing. He said my accent was Mexican. The consulate of El Salvador denied my deportation thinking I was really from Mexico. I did not exist in El Salvador. There were no birth records, no school records, and no medical records. The Salvadorans that had went with me to see the consulate left a few days later, and I was left behind.

The following month the consulate came back again. I was sent to him one last time. Though this time, U.S immigration agents had pressured the consulate to approve my deportation in which the consulate did. As he approved the deportation, he focused on my tattoos and warned me that I was going to have a lot of problems in El Salvador. A few days later I was deported to El Salvador. I was on the airplane, and I was still in disbelief that I was being sent there. It's an episode in my life in which I'd not like to repeat.

I arrived in El Salvador in the middle of 2003. I could not help feeling stupefied as I stood in San Salvador's airport of *Comalapa* with nowhere to go. I found everything strange, the place, the people, the food, the culture. I did not feel strange because I was out in the free world; no, it was because I was out in a distinct world away from mine. All odds were against me, but then again this was not the first time I was going to be the underdog, or the last time. Underdog or not, I was granted a second chance to do something in life, an opportunity that very few get. It was time to start anew, time to start a normal life perhaps even form a family. I could not let this chance slip away. I had all the intentions of making the best of it.

The only person who I was really able to count on was my mother. The rest of my family had grown apart from me while I was in prison. We were just relatives that did not help each other. Quite frankly, I did not give a dam, is less people I have to worry about. My mother however was something else, she has never failed me. She has always been in my corner concern about my everyday scuffles. When she found out I was getting deported she was worried as hell for me.

My grandma had told the story countless times about how she had won the lottery in El Salvador and used that money to take all six of her children to the United States. She also took me, her only grandson born there. All I knew about El Salvador were the stories that were told by my grandma.

She told me that I was born in the province of Santa Ana which is two hours away from the capital of San Salvador. With that in mind, Santa Ana is where I decided to go from the airport. I took a taxi there, to no specific location. When I arrived in the city of Santa Ana I walked around asking people where I was able to find a comfortable hotel. There were many to choose from.

The next day I spent the whole day locked up in the room occasionally sneaking peeks out the door and out the window. The noise of the cars and the crowd of people bothered me, it gave me anxiety. I knew that at one point I had to form part of society, but that was difficult for me to do. I'd sit outside the room watching people walking by and vehicles passing by. When I could not handle the noise any longer I went back inside the room.

Finally, one day I mustered the entire valor I was able to and walked to a nearby mall and sat there doing pretty much the same thing; watching people walk by. I did not know what else to do. I did not know how to live a normal life. I was used of being told when to wake up; when to eat; when to go to shower; when to go to work; and when to go to bed. I wanted to return to prison, but that was the easy way out and my life has always been everything but easy ever since I was born.

When I went out, I just went without worrying too much where I was going. There was no reason to be peculiar about neither the area I was in, nor where I went. I had no enemies as far as I was concern. I wonder hither and tither constantly stopping people along the way to ask questions, or directions. They used words that I had never heard before, and I also used words they were not accustomed to hearing. I would not ask the meaning when they used such words. For, I did not want to appear foreign in the country where I was born. I figure the meanings along the way I thought.

Thus far, everyone seemed hospitable and willing to

help me. Each time I got on a bus, people quickly jumped out of their sit to give to me. And the bus driver refused to take my bus fare, so I'd ride for free. Salvadorans are so generous I thought they do not even want to charge me to ride the bus.

I took pleasure in the small things in life; like looking at live trees and plants, petting an animal, walking at night under the rain, and choosing what food to eat.

One afternoon while I was walking around the mall, I heard a voice from a distance call out: *"hey homie, are you from L.A?"* It was the first time I had heard someone speak English since I arrived in El Salvador. Those words were music to my ears. Douglas had also been deported. He was raised in the west side of Los Angeles. We spent the whole afternoon at his house talking for hours. He explained how life was in El Salvador for us. We had to succumb to living as fugitives secluded away from the public. We are persecuted, jailed, or killed within months of arrival.

I told him where I was staying and to the places where I had walked to. Douglas expressed that I had been very lucky on not been killed. He advised me not to go to those places again. And promise me to help me find a house to rent in a safer place.

I also mentioned to my friend Douglas about the generosity and the willingness the people had shown me; the free service from the bus drivers, and how the people were quick to give me their sits. He laughed and said that the Salvadorans automatically assume that we are members of the *Mara Salvatrucha 13* also known as *MS13* who terrifies the country. Douglas explained that the members of the Mara Salvatrucha do not pay bus fares; in fact they collect working taxes from them. They do not pay entry fees to places that charge them. They do not pay pretty much anything. And if they so desire they can plunder stores without repercussions. They pretty much do as they please. This was my first time hearing about this. I had no idea things were like that in El Salvador.

Douglas offered me to drive me around to the places I need to go, to avoid going out so much. With Douglas I had learned that people were seeing a monster in me. In other words, I was the hobgoblin of the neighborhood. I later found out that the Mara Salvatrucha members did not kill me during the time that I was wondering the streets because they were unsure who I was. They were mistaking me for one of their leaders. They were too frightened to question me. The tattoos on my body had kept me alive when I walked through all those dangerous places Douglas had told me.

That night Douglas took me to a night club where we spent the night drinking and talking about our real home; California. However I could not stop thinking about all the things he had told me. According to him we were doom to become another statistic in El Salvador. If he was aware of this why he was still there, I wondered. He had no intentions of leaving El Salvador. Douglas had accepted his faith already and was not afraid of dying, neither did I, but I was not going to sit around and wait for my demise either.

Douglas helped me find a house just like he had promised. I did not have anything in my new house, only a small mattress that I laid on the floor to sleep on. I spoke with my mother and told her that I had decided to leave El Salvador and head back home. She wanted the same thing for me. I told my friend Douglas that I was planning to head back home.

I left El Salvador after a month of being there. I had no issues getting through Mexico without papers. First I went to Campeche, then to Veracruz, then to Monterrey and finally I arrived to Reynosa Mexico where I enter illegally to the United States. I had never done anything like that before and it felt odd entering the United States illegally. It was like trying to break into my own home. I managed to cross over, but I was detained by border patrol in Laredo Texas. I was charged with "illegal reentry," a crime punishable with up to twenty years in a federal institution. I had no idea of the gravity of that crime. Should I consider myself lucky for receiving a seven-year sentence for crossing the border? A seven-year sentence is what I received. I should be thankful I did not get the twenty-year bid I guess. My arrest did not bother me, not even the seven years I had received for crossing an imaginary line. *"Accustom reconcile us to everything,"* I once read, and it's true. Being in prison did not bother me at all anymore. It had become my way of life for a great part of my existence.

I was first taken to a Correctional Corporation of America, better known as a CCA, in Laredo Texas. CCAs do not belong to the state and do not belong to the federal Government. They are private institutions that get wealthy by housing inmates. They are all over the United States now.

Upon my arrival to the institution, the guards stripped searched me and saw my body covered with tattoos. They asked me where I was from. I told them; California. The officers wanted to lock me away from the general population for my own safety they said, saying that Texan inmates detest Californians. I declined their protection, and I was sent with the rest of the inmates to a housing module. Texans have a different way of running a prison. Their system is based on the strongest feeding off the meek and the weak. There are many prison gangs that exist in the state of Texas. Most of these prison gangs do not get along. Hence, they are kept separately.

When I arrived to the module that I was sent to, I got there with one mindset. And it was to battle with God knows who. I was still physically fit to fight. The last ten years I had spent them exercising daily.

In the module no one told me anything, but I felt the tension when I entered. The following day I went to the recreation yard with other modules. I removed the shirt and wrapped in on my left arm. I did this for two reasons; to identify myself as a Californian by exposing my tattoos, and the shirt on my arm was to be used against any possible knife attack.

I was called over by a group of six. The guy I had in front of me looked like a football player, big corn-fed guy. The ones to my right and to my left did not look so threatening. He asked me where I was from, and I answered. I foresaw the intention of engagement so I threw the first punch. As I did, he lowered his head and I hit him on the forehead. At that moment I did not realized I had fractured two of my knuckles. When the scuffle ended, I had badly injured three of the six. They were sent to the infirmary for stiches. I was sent to an outside hospital for an x-ray and to have a cast placed on my left hand. The fractured knuckles were the only injury that I had suffered, and not a single scratch more.

The story had grown out of proportion by the inmates that had witnessed the scuffle. They had rumored that it was ten against one, and then I heard it was fourteen against one. The last time I heard it was at twenty against one. There were many correctional officers that stopped by my cell to sneak looks. They wanted to see who this mighty person was with their own eyes. They saw me, and could not believe the story. Each time I received a visit from one of those curious officers I'd ask when they were going to release me back to the general population. They did not want to let me out with a cast on my hand, and they had also deemed me a threat to the general population. I was kept there until I was transferred to a federal institution in Three Rivers Texas. I left that CCA with my head held up high. What happened there followed me everywhere I went.

From the moment that I was told by the guards that I was *persona non grata*, I knew that it did not mean I was going to be a victim. Through experience I've learned that being out number or fighting someone much bigger does not mean defeat. Even if, I would have been the injured one, I would have walked away victorious. There's no honor in fighting someone in a group, smaller, or weaker and win, but there's honor in fighting a group, bigger, and stronger and lose.

At *Three Rivers Federal Correctional Institution* there were many inmates from California, Hispanic, Black, and White. They were all united, something that it's not seen in California prisons. The state of Arizona, Colorado, and Utah were our allies. I had no further altercations in federal prison. The environment in those prisons is milder than state prisons.

Federal prisons are the suites of all prisons. Inmates house there are privilege with many things state prison inmates do not have. For example, inside the buildings there were washers and dryers, ice machines, two computers that were used to send out or receive emails from friends and family, there were microwaves, five or six plasma T.Vs with cable channels. The dining area has buffets and the food is good. The recreational yard was immense and provides access to pool tables, fully equipped gyms, with an aerobics or yoga instructor. Also out in the recreation area you can find a mini casino with poker and blackjack tables run by the Italian inmates. Stamps are use as currency. Three stamps equals one dollar, and fifteen stamps is call a "book" which equals five dollars. Time flies by when you are doing a federal prison sentence.

After a year in Three Rivers I was transfer to Lompoc

California which made me happy because I was finally within visiting distance. My mother took advantage of that and went to visit me every chance she got. I also took advantage to take several vocation classes and the G.E.D test at Lompoc. Although I had dropped out of school at twelve-years-old I passed the G.E.D exam with flying colors.

Finally I was transferred to Victorville California which was even closer to home; the visits from my mother were more frequently. And just like that seven years went by, and I grew sad. It was now the ending of 2010. I was schedule to be released once again. When my release day came, they kept calling my name over the loud speaker, over and over, and over, and over again. Some of my fellow inmates went to look for me to tell me that I was being called to the front office to get released. An officer was sent to my cell to escort me out. None were able to find me. I was in the shower taking the longest shower I had ever taken in my entire life. I did not want to be released. The officer finally found me in the shower. He asked me what was wrong with me, if I did not want to go home. I told him I was not going to be sent home. I wished everyone stop saying that. It was too much to explain to him, and I just left it as that.

As I was escorted to the front office some of the fellas came to wish me luck and say their farewells. They said I did not look too happy, and that's because I was not.

CHAPTER 6
UNITED STATES OF CORPORATE AMERICAN AND MODERN DAY SLAVERY

Throughout my lifetime I spent a total of seventeen years locked away in the California Department of Corrections (CDC), Federal Bureau of Prisons (FBOP), and Corrections Corporation of America (CCA).

I've learned many things from all three correctional facilities. Beside from the name they have the same goal in common. That's to generate profit. CDC houses mediocre and violent criminals, FBOP houses white-collar criminals, and CCA house all of the above. The United State has the largest prison population in the world, and second-highest per capita incarceration rate. There's a reason for that.

Prior of going to prison I used to imagine a prison with bars, inmates behind them doing hard time, and rioting. There's some of that, but that's not always the case. Every prison is built with an industry inside that produces a lot of goods and hence, a lot of wealth. In California's prisons the industries are known as *Prison Industry Authority* or simply (PIA). In the federal prisons they are known as *Federal Prison Industry* or simply (FPI) with the trade name of UNICOR. The prisons claim that the inmate is learning a trade to prepare them for the outside world as an excuse to exploit the inmate's labor. It should not be a surprise that prisons are now being privatized by corporations.

Prison industries work under state and federal contracts. Every inmate wants to work for the prison industry, it's the best paying job an inmate can have earning anywhere from twenty-three cents to a dollar and fifteen cents an hour to fulfill contracts that are worth millions of dollars. When a prison goes on lock-down status, industry workers receive special privileges: they are allow to go to work; allow to shower; allow to shop at the prison commissary while the rest of the inmate population remains locked up in the cells. And each time industry workers went on strike, the prison lost a lot of profit.

In many occasions illegal immigrants were allow to work in the prison industry due to the high demand to fulfill contracts. War on terror and war on immigrants bring a lot of fortune to these prison industries. Take for example, FPI in Victorville California, this industry had a contract with the federal government to work on U.S Border Patrol vehicles. Skillful immigrants worked diligently to weld the steel cages inside, tint windows and brand the vehicles with the United States Border Patrol logo. In Three Rivers Texas' FPI inmates were making military garments during the Iraq war.

Another example is in the fabrications of California's car plates. Car plates are made in Folsom's PIA where a team of inmates produce millions of license plates a year. And finally here's a scary example, Victorville California's FPI had a contract to work on military hummers. The hummers had already been in combat. Inmates were paid a bonus of forty dollars for each bullet found in the hummers. A combination of live ammunitions and inmates can only lead to one thing, and that's disaster. That's what occurred in the beginning of 2010.

An inmate that was working in FPI Victorville had a different idea with the live ammunition he was finding in the hummers. Instead of turning them to receive a forty dollar bonus for the ammunition, he was taking them back to his cell. He used the gun power from the ammunition, a radio, a battery pack, and a pen to fabricate an explosive. His target was a Black correctional officer he did not like. He placed the explosive out in the recreation yard by a metal detector early in the morning where the officer was assigned to. He placed four bullet shells from a cal.50 standing upright by the explosive device which appeared to be a radio. Luckily, the officer took precaution. The officer poked the object with his baton. It made a small explosion. The officer could have lost a finger or suffer third degree burns if he had picked it up with his bare hand.

The U.S Marshalls were called to conduct a full investigation. Eventually the inmate responsible was discovered. He was housed in the same building as I. A week prior I had seen the inmate on the dayroom welding the radio (explosive) together. I had asked him what he was working on because he had a bunch of wires and small tools on the table. When I asked him, he said he was making a bomb. I did not take it seriously. That incident of course was never made public. By the way in case you are wondering the individual was not Muslim, he was White.

Slavery and exploitation are the true virtues of the prisons of today, and rehabilitation is just a guise for a lucrative business. Americans are duped into thinking that their wars are created for the good on the country. *Patriotism* is the magical word used to convince Americans, which a bunch of baloney.

PIAs and FPIs could take over the manufacturing enterprise as they build more prisons/industries. If the ensuing of prisons continues, the loss of American jobs dwindles. True, that a prison creates hundreds of jobs for the community, but creates thousands of jobs for inmates, jobs that can be provided to hard working Americans. Do not be fool to think immigrants are the ones taking your jobs.

PROMETHEUS

Prometheus, "the noblest martyr of all Titans?"
Prometheus cursed the world with fire.
Thus it is with fire how we shall retire,
World-destruction is real
And drawing near,

All of us ungrateful humans should begin to fear.
You, others and I will all soon perish,
Cause we could not let go of the gadgets
---- You love to cherish.
We will be burned down with fire,
Turned unto ashes,
Washed away by the ocean splashes.
And should a new breed of species later evolve,
May they learn from our mistakes
---- If is ever solve.

I hope the next species are creature s
From under deep waters and
Away from earth's rotten gutters.
Yet, I wonder how these species would look.
Would they have noses, no noses?

MARVIN E. ORTIZ

Would they even have ears?

Maybe razor-sharp teeth, with scales and gills

That may look like eels?

Or perhaps web-like feet?

Though we will never know, for we will not meet.

CHAPTER 7
SECOND DEPORTATION TO EL SALVADOR

I was deported for the second time in October of 2010 back to El Salvador. I had an idea of how things work there now. I knew the tattoos on my body were a magnet for misfortunes. I also knew that if nothing was done in regards to them, I was doom for failure.

I stayed at the same hotel I did the first time. I kept my tattoos hidden with a long-sleeve shirt and placed some make-up over the ones on my ears and face. I tried to contact my friend Douglas and I learned that he had been murdered in an ambush. He knew something like that was going to happen. He had told me that it was only a matter of time. My friend was right about many things. I followed all his advice I was able to remember. Those were terrible news I had to hear. He was the only in El Salvador that I really trusted.

I went to speak with the man who had rented me the house before, and he was able to accommodate me with a place once again.

Amongst some of the many vocational classes I took in prison was; how to use a computer, how to type, and a Microsoft class. I'm glad I did. All these classes turned out to be useful in my everyday life. I bought myself a laptop and got some internet service. I used that laptop to search for a place where I can remove my tattoos. I found many locations but they were expensive and they were doing a lousy job. They were other clinics that would cut the tattoo off and sew the skin back together. That was out of the question for me, I had too many tattoos. Other clinics where using LASER, but were causing third degree burns.

I spent day and night searching. Finally, I was able to find a place. The equipment they were using was of high technology donated by European countries. Best of all, it was a free program to assist former gang members remove the tattoos so that they may start a new life. There was a six-month waiting period to start the treatment. I patiently waited for my turn.

I caught wind that the some members of the Mara Salvatrucha were asking about me. They wanted to know who was I, and where I had come from? They do this to every newcomer taking special interest on individuals who have family in the United States with the objective to ask for a monthly extortion. In El Salvador it's not recommendable to wear name-brand shoes or clothes. If you do, you're asking for trouble.

If I intended to survive the gang violence in El Salvador I needed to find out more about them and their structure. In the beginning I could not identify its members. They are not the stereotypical gang members I was used of seeing in the Los Angeles with short hair and dressed up in urban clothes. I recalled Douglas words, to always be careful of the young Mara Salvatrucha members because those were the ones that are send for the kill.

Unable to identify its members made me an easy target. I was relying more on instinct than knowledge to stay alive. I had learned to sense danger from long distance in Los Angeles.

My clothing had drawn the attention of the Mara Salvatrucha members. One day a group of young boys of eleven or twelve years old approached me in bikes to ask if I was coming from L.A. I demonstrated no fear, and told them yes. They asked me if I had any tattoos, and I told them yes. They asked if they can see them, and I told them yes. They scrutinized my tattoos searching for any implications that would tie me to their rival gang of Eighteen Street. Their eyes grew when I took off my shirt. The intensity of the tattoos that I was demonstrating - from their perspective - told them I had many kills under my belt. For, the Salvadoran gang members are allowed to get a tattoo only when they have participated in a murder. Implications in murders are defined by the intensity of the tattoos that mark the body. Unlike the United States, gang members in Los Angeles can get a tattoo whenever they like, and as many they like.

They asked me the meanings of the tattoos; I simply told them they were prison tattoos. I knew that they were going to plan my killing they did not seem satisfied with what I had told them. They wanted the meaning of each tattoo, but at least I already had an idea on how they look.

Six months flew by quickly. I had spent those six months like a hermit talking with my mother via live messenger, and also to a good friend of mine I met in Lompoc federal prison; Jeff Cantu from Tampa Bay Florida who had become like a brother to me. They both gave me strength to continue on. I knew that I could not return to the United States. The judge that had sentenced me to seven years warned me that next time he was going to give me fifteen years if I went back. I knew he was not playing. I had met inmates charged with illegal reentry serving a fifteen-year bid.

The first tattoos that I removed were the ones on my face, ears, and neck. Every session consisted of a thirty-minute LASER procedure. I had been placed in a priority list, where I was going every week for a session. It took one month to remove the tattoos on my face, ears, and neck. The process is painful, more painful than having them put on. The pain went beyond physical for me; most of the tattoos were done by special individuals and had been with me for more than two decades. I felt as though I was being amputated. This needed to be done if I had any intentions of living a normal life, and thus I endured.

CHAPTER 8
SALVADORAN GANGS AND THE MISCONCEPTIONS

They are known throughout the world as one of the most violent gangs that have ever existed. The Mara Salvatrucha 13 and Eighteen Street of El Salvador has given a lot to talk about.

They are known as street gangs. In the beginning I had accepted the term "gang" to describe these two groups. After all, the roots of both these groups are from Los Angeles. While in prison, I met members from both gangs and they appeared to have the same principles of most L.A gangs.

Taking my background into account I believe to have a little bit more knowledge about gangs than the average person. In my opinion, I can assert that Salvadoran "gangs" have been erroneously categorized as streets gangs. They are far from being an ordinary street gang. To the naked eye they may seem as primitive Salvadoran gang members. However, the two groups have evolved from a street gang to having a mafia-like structure. Both groups operate in a well organize crime.

The following are factors that distinguish them: Mafias and Salvadoran gangs live of extortions; a L.A street gang does not. Mafias and Salvadoran gangs murder innocent people to carry out vendettas; a L.A street gang does not. Mafias and a Salvadoran gang torture dismember and bag the bodies of their victims; a L.A street gang does not. Mafias and Salvadoran gangs have a ladder within the structure, a pyramid that consists of leaders, advisors, captains, soldiers who are promoted according to killings; a L.A street gangs does not.

Moreover, Salvadoran gangs have taken their atrocities step further by participating in acts of cannibalism, and satanic rituals. The horrendous acts that have been committed by these Salvadoran so-called gangs go against the precepts of any L.A street gang.

The first requirement prior to joining a Salvadoran gang is to commit murder. Hence, in essence every member of a Salvadoran gang is already a killer prior to joining the gang. With this in mind, to say that El Salvador has a "gang problem," is a mistake to say the least.

Salvadoran authorities have not been able to even make a correct assessment about these gangs. Without the correct assessment there will be no solution. Their solution is to point the finger at people like my late friend Douglas and I.

Many members, founders and co-founders from these Salvadoran gangs arrive deported from the United States attempting to put an end to the violence. These individuals try to enforce the precepts of Los Angeles. Not only do the members in El Salvador refuse the idea deeming it as being *weak*, but have murdered their fellow members for attempting to weaken their structure. Though there's something very confounding happening as a result. It's startling, and yet the people are failing to realize what's happening in their own backyard.

MY UPHILL BATTLE

The violence in El Salvador is so terrifying that, even L.A gang members have imagined the country without Salvadoran gangs. Thus, something is being done about this. A prime example is in what happened with the Eighteen Street or (18st) of El Salvador. The effort to end the calamities inflicted on innocent people has forced a division between 18st. It has now broken in two different structures: Eighteen Street Southerners (18st) and Eighteen Revolutionaries (18R). They have become mortal enemies of each other. The Mara Salvatrucha is now adapting the same idea and has divided into: Mara Salvatrucha 13 (MS13) and Mara Salvatrucha 503 (MS503) also have become mortal enemies of one another.

Two internal wars based on different principals. 18st Southerners and MS13 are members fostered in Los Angeles whose goal is to end violence. 18R and MS 503 are members fostered in El Salvador whose goal is to continue their atrocities. 18R and MS503 are members that have never been outside of El Salvador. They are the ones responsible for the killings of numerous innocent people in El Salvador. Note, that the 503 that was added to MS simply means the country's area code. I will not be surprise to later hear that there also MS502 for Guatemalan members, and MS504 for Honduras.

MARVIN E. ORTIZ

CHAPTER 9
ALWAYS BETTER TO CARRY A GUN AND NOT NEED IT, THAN TO NEED ONE AND NOT HAVE IT

I was looking for ways to live in peace, but only because I sought peace does not mean that I did not know how to be violent.

During my youth in Los Angeles I had reason to be careful. I had to be cautious of where I went or where I lived due to gang rivalry. In El Salvador no one has to belong to a Salvadoran gang to be careful where they go. Salvadoran gangs are ready to murder anyone that enters into their territory that they consider a threat. By a threat I mean the simple fact of living in a rival's territory. The victim could be a child, a father, or grandfather. They simply do not care. These gangs presume that they are spies sent by their rivals. That's enough reason to murder an innocent person.

It's a sad situation when there are families that live in two different gangs' territories, and cannot visit themselves due to that. I found out that Salvadoran gangs keep guards on every point of entry in their neighborhood and communicated through conference calls. When a stranger is detected they give notice. Thereupon, the stranger is asked for identification. From the identification they gather the address of where he lives. They ask questions and search the individuals for tattoos. If he so happens to be a salesman he is forced to pay taxes to the members to continue their way. I knew of an old lady that sold fish that declined to pay a two-dollar tax; she was cowardly stabbed by these individuals. Salvadoran gangs are authority, judge, jury, and henchman all at the same time.

The Mara Salvatrucha had already passed judgment on me, of that I was sure. I knew that they were planning to send their henchmen sooner or later, and I was waiting. Trying to appease things with them is useless. They have never understood people like me. They had approached me once already. They did not instill the fear they were looking to instill in me. There was no way I was going to be intimidated by some punk kids. They grow to giants from people's fear. And that would have weakened my position on the board.

Aware of all the terror these Salvadoran gangs are capable, I knew they will not hesitate to kill me and if given the opportunity they will even use me as an asset for a satanic ritual. I had no intentions of being a victim. I had to protect myself by all means. All of the sudden I felt the need to buy a gun. Therefore, I researched how to go about that.

The tattoos on my face, ears, and neck were gone already. I got dressed up with a dress shirt, dress shoes, and dress pants and went to take an exam for a license to carry a weapon. The exam consisted of a written and manual test. The written exam was very basic questions, even for someone that does not know how to read or write their native language well. For the manual exam I was provided a Browning 9mm to disassemble and reassemble, which I did. My picture was taken and I was handed my license for the use of a firearm.

With the license I was able to purchase a weapon. I bought a 1911 Colt .45 with an extra magazine. I carried it with me everywhere I went. Even into places where it was not permitted.

One afternoon while walking home, members of the Mara Salvatrucha tried to make their move on me. I saw three of them walking towards me. I knew those three individuals where on a mission, that I was going to make impossible. They were just kids, no more than fifteen years old perhaps new initiatives to the Mara Salvatrucha trying to earn their bones by killing me. And more than likely they were inexperience, but I was not going to underestimate their capabilities.

Only the youngest one had a gun; a six-shooter. I stood there leaning on a concrete post with my pistol drawn out waiting for them to get closer. I pretended to be looking at a different direction. When they were at about twenty-feet I fired two shots not aiming to hit anyone. All I wanted was to make noise. The sound of the .45 caliber did a nice job of sounding off. The youngster responded by wildly firing six rounds and running. He pulled out scissors, I pulled out rock, lucky for me I did not pulled out paper, or I would have lost.

Due to the incident I had encounter with the Mara Salvatrucha I had to move. There was going to be a next time, and next time they were going to come with real gunslingers. Someone was going to die. In the middle of 2011 I moved to the province of *Metapan*. Metapan is a small town almost four hours away from San Salvador. Metapan is something like the small towns that are seen in the Spanish soap operas; people wearing cowboy hats and boots and riding on horses.

In Metapan I continued living a life like a hermit. Solitude was nothing new to me, but the solitude I was going through in El Salvador was far different than the one I had experience with in prison, and it was taking its toll. Daily I'd go outside in search of food. My accent aroused curiosity that turned into questions I did not like to answer. For instance people would always ask, *"You aren't from around here aren't you?"* I'd just tell them that I was born there.

I was finding adaptation extremely difficult in El Salvador. While all this was happening, I continued to travel to San Salvador weekly for my LASER treatment.

BEAUTIFUL DEATH

I have seen you before, in fact quite often,
You have had chances to take me, but then you soften,
You are nothing like you have been depicted
---- In this hell hole world.
Who would have actually imagined that you are
Such a beautiful girl.

You are not dark and creepy with a hooded head,
But rather brightly sweepy with long jet black hair,
Now that I saw you, I am no longer frighten,
In contrast, I find your company very enlightening.

When will you come? I cannot wait to see you again;
Such beauty, your presence drives me insane,
You are always welcomed to come and pay me a visit,
For a minute, an hour, forever, you will find me enlisted.

MARVIN E. ORTIZ

CHAPTER 10
RESULTS OF EXTREME CULTURE SHOCK

I met other deportees with the same situation but under different conditions. Two cases in particular I cannot forget. Joe was called *"Crazy Joe."* He was from East Los Angeles. Spoke perfectly good English. Although he spoke English and was from Los Angeles, I could never get a conversation out of him. He was about 5'10," slim body frame with a dark complexion. I was able to see he had many tattoos on both his arms, and possibly his neck I could not quite tell because his tattoos were hard to see due to the dirt on his body, and the sun had darken his skin even more than what he naturally was.

Joe had lost his mind in El Salvador. He had lost concept of where he physically was at. When I first met him, I saw him sitting on a sidewalk with a bottle of rubbing alcohol in his hand. The tattoos on his arms were barely visible. I asked him (in English) if he was from L.A. He looked at me with a smile on his face and took a few drinks from the bottle of rubbing alcohol. I asked him again, this time he stood up, laughed, walked away as he loudly yelled; *"I'm from East LA, I'm going back to East LA!"* waving his hands around and tumbling along his way. He startled me when he did that. For, I was not expecting that kind of reaction. I saw him two more times after that and he did the same thing each time, walked away from me on his way to East L.A. He was not like that when he first arrived in El Salvador they told me. El Salvador had turned him that way. I never saw him again. I doubt that he really went back to East L.A. My guess is that he was killed just like many others.

The person that told me about him, he too was deported. His name was Chris. The case of Chris is one in a million. Meeting him made me feel fortunate. Chris was taken to the United States as a toddler. He grew up in a White neighborhood in the suburbs of San Fernando Valley California. Chris even looked Caucasian; tall, slim, light brown hair with hazel eyes. According to him he was a prominent baseball player. Baseball was his passion. In El Salvador he had become a beggar.

Chris understood Spanish, but was unable to speak it. The only thing he had learned how to say in Spanish at the time that I met him was; *"can I have a quarter?"* I met Chris on the bus asking each passenger for a quarter. I gave him two dollars. I was able to tell that he was embarrassed when I spoke with him because his pale-looking face turned red like a tomato. He confessed to me that he desperately wanted to go back to the United States. He had no financial help from his relatives.

My hope of becoming part of the Salvadoran society diminished each time I met a deportee that was struggling as these two were. I had an agenda to follow and I could not put a hold on it simply because I had met someone that had not managed to make a life in El Salvador. The madness of Joe and the desperation of Chris, I found legitimately reasonable. It could have happened to me if I did not have my mother's support and the determination to succeed. These were consequences if I allowed myself

MY UPHILL BATTLE

to deviate from the path I had set upon myself. Succeeding in El Salvador was not going to be a walk in the park, but I could not let myself go like that.

CHAPTER 11
AN ANIMAL'S EYES HAVE THE POWER TO COMFORT

There were times in prison that the only company I had was of a spider or ants. They kept me entertained during their visits. I shared my food with them, and sometimes spoke to them. I think they enjoyed my company as well because they kept coming back to my cell.

You will be surprise how someone can find the company of such small insect like a spider, an ant or even a cockroach comforting in moments when you think you're alone in the world. I found myself alone once again in El Salvador and missing the company of one of those little critters. That's it! Why not go out and get myself a pet. My new friend did not have to be an insect this time. I can go to a pet shop and choose from the many options available there.

My first thought for a pet was a fish, but no I'd have to buy a fish tank with lights and things like that, plus is hard to pet a fish. I'd have to walk to the fish tank every time to spend time with him. I did not want a cat either, I wanted something more manly. A turtle is too slow to keep up. I did not want any type of bird, no caged animals for me. And a snake I could not trust. At the end I did not have to walk into a pet shop. My new best friend was brought to my door by an old man. The old man was holding a white and brown four-month-old American pit-bull terrier that he was selling. He wanted twenty-five dollars for him. I paid the man without hesitation and named the dog after a Stephen King novel; *Cujo*.

Cujo turned out to be indeed the most loyal friend I had in El Salvador. Cujo and I watched T.V and ate together. He slept in my room. He also turned out to be a lucky charm. Shortly after Cujo came into my life I met a woman that was not judgmental, and that did not care about my tattoos or my history. I was happy with the relationship, but Cujo was not. He was jealous. He would growl at her and chase her out the room every time she came to visit me. He stood by the door keeping her away from the room with his teeth showing. She was terrified of the little puppy, and she would not leave my side thinking he was going to bite her any given moment.

An animal has the power to observe all the bad energy, but most importantly animals do not allow opportunity to control their loyalty, men do.

CHAPTER 12
THE FIRST JOB IN MY LIFE

I had no idea what a call center was or what it consisted of. The individual that was working on my tattoos told me that I could find work in one of those places since I spoke perfectly good English. I had nothing to lose; I wrote many résumés and took them to all the call centers I was able to find in San Salvador and there were many.

In the month of December of 2012 I received a call for my first job interview. That was my first one ever in my life. The interview felt more like an interrogation though. It reminded me during the time of my arrest; all the questions. The recruiter asked many questions about my personal life that I found irrelevant. For a brief moment I did not want to be there anymore. He asked; *"where did you learned how to speak English so well?"* I told him I grew up in the United States. He then asked; *"are you deported?"* I answered yes. He asked why, I lied to him by saying that my immigration status was not legal. Then he asked for my consent to do a criminal background check in the United States, which I did not give. What for? They were going to confirm what they already knew, and deny me the opportunity to work anyway.

There was a way to pass the criminal background check I did not know about at that time. All I had to do was say I grew up in Canada. They conduct the criminal background check there, and since I have no records in Canada, the call center does not get any feedback on me. That was the trick deportees were using to get hired.

Boostmobile was bringing their business to El Salvador. A call center by the name of *Teleperformance* was looking into getting the contract. They desperately needed more workers. *Teleperformance* already had contracts with companies like; *Western Union*, *FedEx*, *Kohl's*, *Hilton*, *Cricket*, *AT&T* and many others. They are a prestige multi-million dollar company own by Daniel Julien. Last year (2016) *Teleperformance* revenue $4.050 billion.

I received a call from *Teleperformance*. They asked me to come in for a job interview. I was prepared to say what I had learned in order to pass the criminal background check, though it was not necessary to lie that time. They were too desperate to turn people away. They did not riddle me with questions like the first call center did. They heard my English, tested my English grammar, my typing skills, gave me a month of training and I had the job. And just like the monkey has the ability to swing by its tail, I have the ability to learn rapidly. I became a master in the field.

At the age of thirty-six years old I got a taste of what it's like to earn a living. I was excited about having the job. It was not hard to fulfill what they were asking for. My job consisted of providing customer service to *Boostmobile* customers; provide technical support, and take their credit card or debit card information to process payments. I was earning five-hundred-forty-five dollars a month working forty-five hours a week. It was not a whole lot I was earning. It was peanuts for a company like *Teleperformance*, but it was enough for me and Cujo to get by on. It was an easy way to earn a living; above all I was beginning to have a social life. Working in an environment where everyone spoke English was ideal for me. The place made me feel like home: back in California. Peculiarly many of my colleagues had come from urban areas of California, Texas, or New York; former gang members and ex-convicts. Who could have imagined we are the representatives to most big companies' customer service. We had a lot in common.

Every day I'd travel three and a half hours to get to work, and another three and a half hours to get home. I could not afford to move to San Salvador with the pay I was receiving. Traveling back and forth every day was difficult, but everything is difficult at first. Working for *Teleperformance* kept me away from sitting at home lamenting on being in El Salvador. If I was not at work, I was on the bus going to work or coming from work. Before heading off, I'd leave the T.V on for Cujo. I left it on his favorite channel- *Animal Planet*.

When I got home from work, Cujo always greeted me the same way, by running back and forth jumping up and down attempting to kiss me. He was always glad to see me get home safe. The wagging of his tail spoke to me in a loud tone.

During the three years that I worked there, I saw things that were not appealing to me. I had to get use of the ridicules that were made on Black *Boostmobile* customers. The representatives would ridicule their names and the way they spoke. They were regarded as the beggars of credit, as far as *Boostmobile* was concern. Black males were given the name of "Tyrone" and Black females the name of "Shiniqua." With these names credit callers were identified. Credit calls from Tyrone or Shiniqua were considered the most difficult calls to handle, and they were the most common. Those calls almost ended up escalated to a supervisor.

At work I had become an excellent representative due to my natural ability to communicate with Black customers. I knew how to deescalate the matters, made them understand that there were things that could not be done. I became so good at this that each time a customer requested to speak with a supervisor; I was call upon to take over the call and I was not even a supervisor. Talking to Black customers and hearing their name was nothing new to me. In fact, I took pleasure on our brief conversations. I had grown amongst them and as far as I'm concern, we belong to the same underdog team in life.

I never expressed my discontent about the ridicules the company made to my superiors. For, most of the ridicules came from my superiors. The call center was my refuge and I did not want to make it a miserable place for me to work in so I kept quiet about this.

If only customers knew that the person they were giving out their credit or debit card information was located in El Salvador, with gang tattoos that had come out of a gritty urban neighborhood, or prison. Maybe I would not have that job. I could have easily jotted down their information and use it for my personal benefit, like many others had done in the past, but it never crossed my mind.

The company did not care where I had come from. All the company cared about is that I spoke good English, have an easy manner and quick to please the customers. *Teleperformance* is a lifeline for many ex-felons who have been booted from the United States for committing criminal acts. Next time you call customer services ask where you are calling to, who knows you might be talking to me.

CHAPTER 13
EL SALVADOR, THE MURDER CAPITAL OF THE WORLD

Almost six years had passed by and I was still alive in El Salvador. I was finally adapting to the place. However, the violence in El Salvador was escalating. By 6pm the streets turn into ghost towns.

Society lives with a constant fear, and due to the ambiguity of the laws there's very little that they do to protect themselves.

In the month of June of 2016 there was seven-hundred murders reported in El Salvador, and in the month of August of 2016 there were nine-hundred murders. There's a murder every hour in El Salvador, a country of a population of 6.3 million. The violence had skyrocketed since my arrival. The gangs sought a truce at one point, but it did not last long.

The discrepancies that exist within the law do not help the situation either. Laws favor the criminal. For instance, I had the right to bear an arm, but it's illegal to use it against someone that threatens my life, or my property. Not even an officer is allowed to shoot a culprit until the culprit fires a weapon first. An officer does not get off the hook like in the United States by simply claiming he feared for his life. The justice system does not allow for the minor to get trial as an adult no matter the gravity of the crime. For this reason and others, minors are use as hit men. In addition, El Salvador refuses to introduce the death penalty for murder with special circumstances. The lack of the death penalty has caused the prisons to overcrowd. They are overcrowded with Ted Bundy, Charles Manson-like inmates that have nothing else to lose. These vermin continue to give out orders to carry out killings on innocent people. If they are caught and link to a murder, another twenty-five years are added to the already two-hundred plus year sentence. It's a meaningless sentence. Subsequently the hits go on.

Not everyone is taking the Salvadoran gang terror lightly. There are many angry sons, fathers, brothers and patriots that have grown tired of the justice system and the violence therein. It's at times like this that drastic measures are taken, and death squads are form with angry victims that are eager to join them.

I must say that I found the idea of vigilante justice extremely attractive. I appealed to the idea of hunting down a monster that has done evil to an innocent person. Nothing would bring me more pleasure than to help defenseless and hardworking people in society. The people of El Salvador feels the same way, they have embraced these want-to-be real life heroes known as the *Sombra Negra* or the *Black Shadow*. They love the idea of having someone who terrorizes gang members at night. I too had grown tired of these want-to-be L.A gang members imposters that have blemished the image of L.A gangs. They've given us all a bad name. L.A gang members are not saints, though we are not monsters who terrorize defenseless people either.

The *Sombra Negra* is not something new. They existed in the early 1990s. They came to exist for the same reason, to eliminate gang members. And it worked, to a certain extent. For a long time these gangs went underground. They were back now and stronger than ever before.

The whole country knows about the *Sombra Negra*, but denies their existence. They deny their existence to keep Human Rights away from the situation. As I said, society loves the idea of having these real life super heroes around. The *Sombra Negra* hunts down anyone who they believe to be a gang member. They act upon a general profile they have adopted not realizing the profile has a wider spectrum causing them to murder individuals that have no ties to these Salvadoran gangs.

I so happened to fit right in that profile and you can only imagine how many individuals deported from the United States fitted right in. The government and mainstream media has always pointed the finger at deportees. The *Sombra Negra* is acting on that accusation by executing and taunting deportees with impunity, and I was on their list.

CHAPTER 14
TENDENTIOUS LAWS ARE RESULTS FOR INCOMPETENCE

In the beginning I did not know why I was being followed, or by whom. This was before I knew about the existence of *Sombra Negra*. It was always the same vehicle trailing me, a new white Toyota Hilux with tinted windows. The pickup obviously drove around with special privilege. In El Salvador it's illegal to have the front window of a vehicle tinted completely black.

I always saw the vehicle during the morning on my way to work. It went in circles. No one likes to be followed like that, at least not me. So I started taking my weapon to work. I placed the pistol and the extra magazine in my backpack. Best to be judge by twelve than to be carry by six. I took the weapon to work for two months. Then I had to stop. Surprisingly I found out at work that security was going to start searching all of the bags that when inside the building. Metal detectors were being installed throughout the work premises also. There was no way for me to sneak the pistol in the working premises. I was left with no choice but to stop taking the weapon to work. Nevertheless, I always took the fire pin with me.

I mentioned the white pick-up that followed me around to some of my co-workers. Apparently, white pick-ups were not the only ones trialing people; there were also green and grey ones of the same make and model, all with tinted windows which were operating across the country. They were detectives, ex-military, and civilians. There were death squads.

I had been so engrossed with work that I was not paying attention of what was happening around me. I did not watch the local channels as I should have been doing. I only watched all English channels; *KTLA*, *ESPN*, and the *History Channel*. The local channels were reporting a war I was not aware of between Salvadoran gang members and authority. Murders committed with glamour; bodies found in bags, suitcases, many times dismembered.

I was warned by some of my colleagues to be very careful because there were some representatives from *FedEx* and *Hilton* that had been murdered by these mysterious Toyotas with tinted windows in recent months.

One night when I came home from work I was surprised by Cujo reaction. Upon opening the door to my house Cujo ran out onto the streets. I took off after him shouting his name. When I finally got a hold on him, I tried to bring him inside the house; he did not want to go in. I had to force him inside. He went under a table and was shaking terribly. I pulled him out from beneath the table to see what was wrong with him. I found two bloody spots on his back, as though he had got Taser.

I looked around the house as though someone was still there. I was able to see that someone had moved items around my house, and carefully tried to place them back like they originally were. To me it was obvious someone had entered my house. Whoever they were it appeared to me that these individuals took special interest on my prison photo album, and possibly took copies of my pictures. I could tell the pictures were pulled out because the pictures no longer stayed in place on the sticky pages.

I was became very upset and worry at the same time. I did not like the idea of been targeted especially if I did not know who was targeting me. What were they looking for? There was a possibility that it could have been a burglar that knew I was gone most of the day or the Mara Salvatrucha. But no, it was neither a burglar nor the Mara Salvatrucha. The intruders were the *Sombra Negra*. Besides, the Mara Salvatrucha and the burglar would have taken my jewelry, cash money, and my pistol all which I always kept in my drawer in plain view. All the items were still there. The intruders definitely wanted something else, they wanted me.

I went for my gun, put the firing pin in place, and when I mounted a round in the chamber the hammer did not held in place. The hammer came down as I released it and a shot was fired. The bullet hit the floor about two feet away from where I was standing. I could have easily shot myself if I hadn't been careful. I swiftly unloaded the weapon. I cocked the hammer back and released it many times. The hammer came down each time. It was no longer staying in place.

I disassembled the weapon to further inspect it. What I saw thereupon really pissed me off. Someone had run a file on the lower part of the hammer that holds it in place. Someone deliberately altered the firing mechanism of my gun. Evidently these individuals wanted me to have an accident by shooting myself.

I was living in a small residential area where there were gatekeepers in the front entry. My house was located by the entrance. I rushed out the house to speak to one of the gatekeepers that I knew well. In spite of all the anger I was feeling at the moment, I was able to suppress it and politely spoke to the gatekeeper. I told him that I knew someone had gone inside my house, and asked him to tell me who they were, and why were they entering my home.

This gatekeeper knew I was a working man, he knew I was not part of the Mara Salvatrucha. I emphasized that I had nothing to hide. In the event that it was the authority wanting to conduct an investigation on me or search my house they were more than welcome to do so in my presence. The face expression on the gatekeeper worried me. He lowered his head and mumbled the words *"get out of here, they're after you."* I wanted to ask more questions but I held back thinking he was already risking his life to warn me. His expression and words could not have been clearer to me. He did not have the need to say anymore: the *Sombra Negra* was after me, and I needed to leave. I did not sleep much that night and neither did Cujo. I was able to repair the gun the same day. I placed it underneath the pillow that night, and every night that follow thereafter.

At work I was no longer performing well. I could not concentrate anymore. I could not stop thinking that someone could be inside my house at that very moment harming Cujo, and waiting for me to get home to torture me, and kill me. I could see the fear in Cujo's eyes each morning as I got ready to head to work. I tried my best not to lose control of myself. A few days later I found out that, military personnel were occupying the houses next to mine. The individual that told me was murdered shortly after, shot dead at a body shop where he worked.

Every night I arrived home expecting to be killed. I had accepted the fact that a group of professional killers were going to try and kill me. I just hoped that if it occurs it would be a swift death. I did not stand the thought of being torture. I had saw images on the web of tortured gang members that were posted by the death squad. I did not have peace of mind thinking of all that was happening. I was being taunted. My girlfriend, Gabriela was becoming very concern also. I kept her away from the house, for her own safety.

I'm convinced that the *Sombra Negra* found grounds

to justify my killing in the pictures they had seen in my photo album. The album contained many pictures I had taken with some of my fellow prison comrades from all over California. My tattoos as well as the tattoos of my comrades were visible. There were also some pictures that I had taken with members of the Mara Salvatrucha. I had taken those pictures with members of the Mara Salvatrucha as a sign of solidarity. Prison vines people together to have a strong solidarity with their roots. A way to demonstrate solidarity in prison is by taking group pictures with fellow countrymen. It does not mean that I am member nor was a member of the Mara Salvatrucha, no way. Those pictures had no other significance. I had had those pictures for decades, and they were now haunting me. At that moment I was feeling so upset that I tore my photo album with all of the pictures inside including the ones of my family as if that was going to erase my past.

It was only a matter of time before the *Sombra Negra* came for me. My intentions were to go out with a blast, and I got ready for that. I quitted my job, I went out to purchase a box of ammunition, filled my refrigerator with beer, and I sat at home with a beer in one hand and my 1911 Colt .45 in the other hand waiting for those bastards to come knocking my door down. I wanted to announce it that I was ready for the party. Yet, somehow they must've known that.

On January 12th of 2016, while I took Cujo out for a walk they tried to make a move on me. I walked with my weapon on my waist band, the extra magazine, and more ammunition in my pocket. It was about 6pm. There was a bit of rain that afternoon. The streets were lonely as usual. I took a one-way road that's surrounded by coffee plantations on both sides of the road. I noticed the white Toyota with the tinted windows that passed by me. It went around, and a few minutes later it passed me by again. I cocked the hammer on my pistol and continued walking.

The pick-up came back for the second time already, but this time it stopped to my left side at a distance of about thirty feet. I stopped for a few minutes to see if someone was going to get out. No one stepped outside the vehicle, but rather another white Toyota Hilux with tinted windows pulled up to my right side about twenty feet.

There were now two idle pick-ups there standing before me in a tactical position, one to my right the other to my left. They had planned this out it seemed like. I waited for a few minutes to see what their next move was. I know what they wanted, they wanted for me to walk between the two pick-ups. They had a ten feet distance between themselves possibly to avoid friendly fire.

This people had altered my pistol and had Taser Cujo I became upset of the thought of this. I started to walk towards the first pick-up to encounter it, but I paused after a couple of steps recalling; straightforward actions normally lead to engagement. In a different time I would have lost my temper and walk right in between the two taking shots at them, which is what they wanted. I did not think the same anymore. I remember; *"On hemmed-in ground, resort to stratagem, on desperate ground, fight."* I was not on desperate ground yet. Their forces were superior and united, therefore I needed to evade and separate in order to weaken them. These were strategies I had read about before and now I was putting them into practice.

I wanted to get things over with already. But it would have been foolish of me to walk into their trap. I was going to make things more difficult for them. If they wanted me that bad they would have to follow me inside the coffee plantation where I had better leverage. I was going to make it as difficult as possible for them to accomplish their goal. They were not going to parade my corpse as a trophy and place before-and-after pictures of me online like they had done with other victims.

Cujo and I climbed about ten or fifteen yards up a hill. I had a good view of the road from up there. The white Toyota pick-up that was on left made a reverse to the area where I had climbed. I squatted there watching what their next move was. My trigger finger itched but I held back the urge to fire. The other white Toyota pick-up had gone around to intercept me on the other side of the hill. I went further into the coffee plantation. I tightly held my pistol in one hand and Cujo's leash in the other stumbling a few times along the way. It was quickly getting dark and the rain was coming in stronger. The rain kept fogging up my glasses and I had to take them off in order to see well. My vision was a total blur. Cujo was slowing me down, for a split second I thought of unleashing him but I did not want to lose him.

His white spots also made him visible in the dark. I tried to camouflage the white areas on his face and back with mud, but he kept shaking the mud off of him. I heard some rapid shooting. They were carrying semi-automatics with silencers. They had used a silencer to kill someone I knew in San Salvador. They were using silencers to avoid drawing attention to them, I assumed.

The sound of a .45 caliber makes enough noise to bring attention of the locals or authority. I decided to let out three rounds in an attempt to draw the attention of local authority, maybe the sound of sirens will scare this people away I thought. Nevertheless, the authorities never show up after I unloaded the three rounds. They were the authority! I quickly replaced the rounds I had fired back into the magazine from the extra bullets I carried in my pocket.

Cujo and I kept moving as quickly as we could further up. I found an area where the dirt was loose enough to dig a foxhole. I dug a foxhole as quickly as I could and cut my hands with sharp fragments as I dug the hole. I did not feel any pain at the time; I just kept digging as fast as I could. I dug the foxhole big enough for Cujo and me to hide in.

Cujo was the first to go inside. He knew something

was wrong and I tried my best to calm him down by talking to him. He laid there not making a sound. I felt them coming closer, one of them passed right by where I was at. I could have shot him and took his weapon if I wanted, but I contained myself. I did not want to kill anyone unless I had to. They were not able to find us.

All of the sudden I heard cat noises coming from different directions. It was them making the noise. These individuals knew Cujo well. They knew that he barked at the sound of cat noise. I thought for sure Cujo was going to give us up with his loud bark. I was dumbfounded to see him just laid there with frighten eyes and dirt all over his face. He appeared to be more scared than I. We remained idle the whole night.

Early the next day, we came out the hiding place. I had dirt all over; in my hair, in my ears, and inside my pockets. I removed the dirt as best as I could, and Cujo shook his off also. I noticed the cuts in my hands. I was starting to feel some pain from the wounds on my hands now. I searched for my glasses to put them back on but they were nowhere to be found. I had lost them during the pursuit. I knew that I needed to get out the country, or wait for this to happen again. I called Gabriela (my girlfriend) to let her know what had happened. She quickly arrived to my house and was determined to stay by my side no matter what. Frankly, I was happy to hear that. I needed the company of someone else to help me think straight.

We were going to need all the money we could gather to travel. In cash I had close to five-hundred dollars at home. I pawn all my jewelry; a chain with medallion, two rings, and bracelet, and I sold the pistol. First thing I did with that money was rented a car. Gabriela and I went to get our passports. We drove to all the agencies we could find searching to find one that would allow us to travel with a dog. We did not want to leave Cujo behind. There were no agencies that allowed pets to travel on board. I tried to contact different people that I knew to see if they can care for Cujo while I came back for him. Funny how *friends* tend to disappear at times like this. I left Cujo with the only person I was able to contact. Cesar is a dog lover himself. I knew he was going to take good care of Cujo.

That night Gabriela and I spent it in a motel. We had purchased tickets to travel to *San Jose* Costa Rica. We were scheduled to leave the following day (January 14, 2016). I left all my belongings behind. It did not hurt me to lose all the material stuff I had worked so hard on getting, what made me woeful throughout my trip was leaving my best friend behind. I vowed to myself that I was going to return for him. I did not know how I was going to do it, but it was going to get done; of that I was sure.

What makes this situation very peculiar is that the *Sombra Negra* resurrected after the former mayor of New York Rudy Giuliani became a consultant on Salvador Sanchez Ceren's (current president of El Salvador) Council on Citizen Security.

Giuliani became involved in the ending of 2015. He intends to reduce crime in El Salvador by putting into practice *The Broken Windows Theory*. In 2016 he was going to send a group of experts that specializes in gangs. He mentioned that the team of experts was going to "quietly" operate in the streets with Salvadoran officials and possibly meet up with former gang members. In other words, he was going to work with informants. It does not surprise me to find out if some of the people I knew from the call center and in my social life were sympathizer of Mr. Giuliani's team. There are individuals in El Salvador willing to say anything for a miserable dollar. Throughout the six years that I lived in El Salvador I met lots of people that shared my same background. However, that did not mean anything. You can laugh with many, but do not ever trust in any. El Salvador has turned homeboys into humbugs, and men into pansies.

Giuliani also made a chilling statement that I believe he literally is doing. According to a simultaneous Spanish-language translation of his remarks he said; *"The biggest problem in New York was the mafia and then drug traffickers, but here it's two major gangs, and these two gangs need to be annihilated,"* This explains the presence of the *Sombra Negra*. Coincidence, I think not.

MY UPHILL BATTLE

MY MOTHERLAND

I abandoned you a long time ago
---- When I was only one year.
You witnessed my birth and off I was gone,
I trade you; my motherland for the so-called dream,
That never came, it went downstream.

Thirty-five years after and I'm back with you,
You take me in, but make me feel blue.
You speak to me in a different language,
I do not understand----
You show some anguish.

For, I was reared by a far-away culture,
That turned out to be a blood-sucking vulture,
Yet, I will now leave; here I am not wanted,
The things I seek most are not here to be granted.

Maybe one day I will return, when I am most needed,
If I hear you cry----
I promise that you will not go unheeded.

CHAPTER 15
PROBLEMS AT THE GUATEMALAN BORDER

We arrived at the Guatemalan border about 9am. Two Salvadoran customs got on the bus we were traveling in. No one was told to step out the bus, no one with the exception of Gabriela and me. Each one of us was taken to separate offices. The officer asked me for my passport. He scrutinized it as if it was false. He asked me; where was I going; why was I heading there; and why was I leaving the country in such a rush, he also asked if I was running away from someone which I thought of as an odd question. The officer kept asking me the same questions in different terms. This lasted nearly an hour.

In the other office, Gabriela was asked the same thing; if I was running away from someone. They asked us to pull out our handbags from the bus. They went through our belongings. I was beginning to think that we were not going to be allowed to leave the country. I thought they were going to detain me and turn me in to the authorities, and authorities were going to turn me in to the death squad that had been after me, which is the authority.

I was not going to let that happen. I was going to fight them off and run towards Guatemala. Central American officials generally are not huge and robust like American officials are. They are small, slender and malnutrition. At thirty-nine years of age, I still felt strong and very capable of putting a fiercely fight. The streets of Los Angeles had taught me how to survive and prison had transformed me into a fighting machine.

The bus driver was getting annoyed by the delay the officers were causing. They were holding the bus back. He kept reminding customs that he had a schedule to follow. Reluctantly they allowed us to get back on the bus and continued the trip to Costa Rica. We went through Guatemala and passed through Honduras with no further issues. We spent a night in *Managua* Nicaragua. The following afternoon, we arrived in San Jose Costa Rica.

CHAPTER 16
FAILURE IN COSTA RICA

We were relief to finally arrive in Costa Rica. I felt a huge weight had been lifted off my shoulders. The scenery on the way to San Jose is beautiful, surrounded by tropical trees and you can still find people who rode their horses in the small towns, very similar to Metapan. I saw this as yet another opportunity to start anew in search of a peaceful life. I was not asking for a whole lot.

I was optimistic about Costa Rica. I always thought of Costa Rica as the second-land of opportunity, United States being the first. Their culture supposed to be more modernized and civilized. I automatically thought this made the country more hospitable. Though modernization and civilization does not make the countries hospitable, in contrast, it makes the people arrogant.

My goal in Costa Rica was to first legalize my immigration status, and then apply to work for the same company I was working for in El Salvador –*Teleperformance* – doing the same thing, providing customer assistance to *Boostmobile* customers. *Teleperformance* has a branch in San

Jose Costa Rica and they too have a contract with *Boostmobile*.

Upon our arrival to San Jose we took a taxi to a hotel. I paid the hotel for a week of service where we relaxed the rest of the day. We were incommunicado with our families. Neither of us had brought a cellphone thinking it was not going to work in another country. The cellphones were left behind with Gabriela's family. Our first objective was to purchase a cellphone so that we may communicate with our families and let them know where we were. I had not mentioned anyone outside of El Salvador where I was going. I did not want to worry my mother. First thing in the morning we sought a store where we could purchase a cellphone. As we walked in search for a store Gabriela noticed that the people gave us hostile glares. When we asked where we could find a store, they responded with a hostile attitude. They pretended not to know the things we asked. The ones that did answer our questions intentionally misdirected us.

We finally found a cellphone store. I asked for prices but was told the phones were not for sell. Imagine being told by a cellphone store that the phones in display were not for sell. To me it was a slap in the face and I felt like punching the salesman in the face but I just walked away avoiding any kind of confrontations in a country where I was searching for peace.

I saw a taxi pass by and I waved it down. I asked him to drive us to an immigration office. He asked us where we from and I told him, El Salvador. The driver drove around, and around, pretending he did not know where the office was. Taxis in Costa Rica run on a meter. They are taxi sharks. He drove me around but did not take me to the immigration office as I had asked him to. He told me he did not know where that was located. Still, the prick wanted me to pay him. In which I did not pay. It almost turned into a scuffle. Costa Ricans had annoyed me in just two days of me being there.

We had no communication with our families. My mother did not know where I was. I chastised myself for choosing to come to Costa Rica without doing any research about the country first. I expressed my frustration to Gabriela, she too sounded disappointed. Now I understood why Nicaraguans spoke so badly about them. Costa Ricans are racist. They regard themselves as superior to other Central American countries. I had arrived in Costa Rica with a false perception. It took us two days in Costa Rica to notice we were not going get the help I was looking for. We had no other choice but head back the same way we came in, through Nicaragua.

CHAPTER 17
HOMIES OR HUMBUGS, THEY ARE ALL OVER THE WORLD

During the trip back to Nicaragua I felt deterred and disappointed. I had no back-up plan. We rode the bus not knowing where we were headed. We ended up in a place call *Barrio Bolonia* in Managua. The houses looked very much that same as the ones in El Salvador small and deterred. The streets were of dirt roads and dark. It did not look like a safe place. It's not a place where I want to live, at least not in Barrio Bolonia. The people in Nicaragua were more hospitable than their neighboring country of Costa Rica. They were very helpful in providing information. Third-world countries, or "uncivilized" countries whatever you want to call them, are more hospitable and the people are quick to help.

At night Gabriela and I took a walk in search of something to eat. As we walked, I saw an individual heading our way. He did not have a good presentation, thus I went on alert mode. He looked homeless. He waived at me with both hands. When he got closer he smile and he spoke in native English. His had a funky smell mixed with alcohol. He was missing a front tooth. Definitely he was an alcoholic, perhaps a drug addict though that was none of my business.

He was a homie from Orange County California. He reminded me of *Crazy Joe*, but this one still had a concept of reality. I had seen many homies under the same condition in El Salvador victims of a traumatic culture shock. Drug addict, alcoholic, thief or not, he was in the same boat as I; marooned in a strange world that was not our own. The joy he felt when he saw me was evident to me. It was the same joy I used to get each time I met someone from the United States in El Salvador. There we were, a homie born in Nicaragua and myself born in El Salvador understanding each other gestures and jives. There were more in common between us two, than what we had in common with our own countrymen.

I told him the situation El Salvador was undergoing. His advice was to head north, to Guatemala where there were better opportunities. He confirmed that Nicaragua was not a good place to live. Not because of the danger but due to the lack of opportunities. The poverty in Nicaragua is far worse than the poverty in El Salvador. I took his advice and headed north. Before I left he asked me if I was able to spare a few Córdobas so that he can buy himself a drink. I gave him fifty Córdobas which is less than two American dollars.

My next stop was in *San Pedro Sula* the Coastal area of Honduras. San Pedro Sula is a beautiful city unlike any other. The area is heavily populated with Afro-Honduras. Most of them ware dreadlocks and look like Bob Marley. In the street lights you can find them dancing and performing acrobats as a way of earning a living.

Prior to arriving in San Pedro Sula, I met a Frenchman in Honduras capital of *Tegucigalpa* that worked as a chef in Paris. The Frenchman was on his way to *Roatan Island* which is located off San Pedro Sula. We rode the same bus there. The Frenchman smelled like cigarettes, he was a constant smoker. He had long hair and a badly shape beard. He did not look like a chef, but then again he was the first French chef I had met.

The Frenchman and I were able to communicate using his broken down English and my terrible French. This was not his first trip to San Pedro Sula, he knew the area well. Roatan Island was a place where he liked to vacation. He advised me that we should share a room at the hotel in order to save up some money. I agreed.

It was already late when we arrived to San Pedro Sula. He invited us to dinner. We walked to a place where they sold *"baleadas,"* a typical Honduras dish that we enjoyed very much. I explained to him the motive that had brought me to San Pedro Sula. He offered to help Gabriela and me if we decided to head to Paris. I loved the thought of that, but I knew that was not going to happen.

When we arrived to the hotel Gabriela did not want to share the room with the strange Frenchman. She was frightened by him thinking he was going to attack me and have his way with her. She did not sleep much that night. I did not sleep much either, she kept waking me up all night each time the Frenchman moved in his bed. She even when to the extent of sleeping with an extra pair pans that night. I thought she was over doing it, but she really was scared.

The following morning my initial thought of the Frenchman was confirmed, he did not like to shower. He had not shower upon our arrival to the hotel, and did not shower in the morning before heading out. Regardless, he was an okay guy. To me that did not matter. I had met people in suits who shower three times a day and that did not make them good people either. In the morning the Frenchman again invited us to eat. We took the invitation but this time I insisted on paying the bill. We ate *"baleadas"* again.

CHAPTER 18
BACK IN GUATEMALA WITH A NEW PLAN

From San Pedro Sula we traveled to *Puerto Barrios* Guatemala, and then took another bus to the capital of Guatemala, finally we arrived to *Petén* Guatemala. We spent the whole day traveling that day. We found a comfortable hotel in Petén. It was in Petén where I was finally was able to purchase a cellphone. The first person I contacted was my mother. I had not spoken to her since I left El Salvador. I told her some of the things that were happening in El Salvador without going into too much detail.

    She did not seem surprise to hear that, she was expecting for something like that to happen sooner or later. The *Sombra Negra* has a bad history in El Salvador. In a way she was glad I had left. She never liked the idea of me living in El Salvador in the first place. She always wanted for me to be closer to her. She had mentioned me many times before that she wanted for me to move to *Tijuana*. She could visit me there at least once a year. I had been in El Salvador for six years and never got a visit from her. I have not seen her in more than six years. The last time I saw her was only for a few hours, when I was still in prison.

I never have been Facebook frenzy. Though I thought this was a perfect opportunity to make use of that famous outlet. I started to search for some of my childhood friends. I managed to find some and sent them all a friend request. Someone was going to be happy to hear from me, at least that what I hoping.

Gabriela and I were stuck in *Santa Elena*, Petén without a back-up plan. In spite of being in a beautiful, magical, enchanted Mayan city I could not help feeling depressed. Across the bridge from Santa Elena there's an island called *Las Flores*. In that island we spent most of our time contemplating what we were going to do next. Petén is best known for the temple of Tikal, thus you can find a lot of tourists from all over the world there. I thought that perhaps I could find a job at a hotel to earn a little bit of money while we figure out what we were going to do. I went to every hotel in the island asking for a job thinking that maybe they can use someone that spoke English. I was turned away by all of them. The receptionist all spoke good English; most of them were foreigners and owner of the hotels.

Every day we would go to the island and sit along the water to watch the fishes swim around while the tourists walk by us. We would buy food and eat in the island. The island was good to the homeless, they were surrounded by water which provided a place to bathe and groom. There were many homeless in the island including some that had come as far as Belize. There were many restaurants along the island that threw away untouched food, which the homeless foraged. There were some homeless that had made flooding huts and lived inside of them. The homeless have a unique life without belonging here or there and without boundaries. I pictured myself doing the same thing, but I was not traveling alone. I had to take care of Gabriela.

A week in Guatemala passed by, and I finally heard from one of my homeboys. This homeboy of mine was born in Belize but was living in San Francisco California. Petén is border with Belize. It's less than a half hour away. He mentioned his brother was in *Corozal*, Belize, and told me to head there. He was going to speak with his brother, get his number so that I can call him when I was there. So off we went to *Melchor de Mencos*, the Belizean border. What a mistake that turned out to be. Belizean customs did not allow Gabriela and me to enter the country.

They say we were not carrying enough money to spend in the country. What they were really looking for was for me to offer a bribe to allow us in, which I did not offered. I called my homeboy in San Francisco California several times, but he did not answer. We had travel to Belize in vain. I went back to Petén upset. I think I would have bopped my homeboy over the head he was before me at that time. I never heard from that dimwit again.

Funds were getting low. I needed to do something to generate money. Gabriela had the idea to sell some of the clothes we had brought. It really was not a bad idea at all. We were carrying too much weight, more than the necessary. In the beginning, I do admit, that I was a bit hesitant to walk the streets of Petén with clothes in hand offering it to people. I had never done anything like that before. I was carrying good clothes. My clothes were sent to me from the United States and they were in good condition, almost new. Guatemalans love American brands like Levis, Tommy Hilfiger, and Polo. We had no problem selling all of the clothes. I turned out to be a good salesman after all. I've never told my mother what I did. She had sent me that clothes, and I sold it at a cheap price.

During that same week I heard from my homeboy *Bad Boy* who was now a Christian, my homeboy *Yankee* who was a construction worker in Colorado, my homeboy *Lonely* who was a supervisor for *UPS*, and my homeboy *Joker*. They narrated their life of two decades in a few hours of conversation, and I told them mine. All of them great fathers and some even grandfathers. Time sure flies by. My story was short, with not much to say, seventeen years of my life were dead years. The rest of the years consisted of struggles searching for a place to start a new life. I was not asking for a whole lot out of life.

We had been out of touch for more than two decades, and our mutual respect and comradeship was of yesterday. I felt over joy to hear the voice of old comrades. They are survivors from the worst era of the streets of South Los Angeles. My homeboy *Chuyin* and *Cricket* were also quick to extend a hand out to me.

Frankly, I was not expecting the help of so many. *Bad Boy* would call me every night to check up on me. He told me God had a plan for me and the things that were happening to me were only God's will. I did not believe him and did not believe God had a will for me. The course of my life was predetermined by something else, a curse maybe.

Despite of my disbelief, *Bad Boy* provided the sustenance I needed to keep pushing forward. All of my homeboys encouraged me to head to Mexico. And they were right. Mexico is where I should have head from the beginning. During my first deportation to El Salvador, they were refusing to take me because they accused me of being Mexican. In El Salvador some doubted my nationally, in short, everyone I speak with seems to think I'm from Mexico. I was not going to have a problem traveling through Mexico. I had done it before, but Gabriela was something else. She was bound to have issues.

The following days and nights I spent them teaching

Gabriela how to speak with a Mexican accent, taught her some Mexican culture and geography. One of my homeboys sent me two Mexican birth certificates, one for her and the other for me. She was able to memorize all the information on the birth certificate: her new name, parent's name, grandparent's name, place of birth and birthdate. A week of practice went by and she still had the Salvadoran accent. Two weeks went by and she still had that accent. I was asking her to do something that's not feasible to do in such a short period of time. I lived in El Salvador for six years and my accent never changed.

We were running out of money, I had no other choice but to travel with Gabriela with what I had taught her. She would have to give it her best shot at the Mexican border; and let the chips fall where they may. We could not afford to stay in Guatemala any longer. We had to move soon.

MARVIN E. ORTIZ

CHAPTER 19
AT THE MEXICAN BORDER OF TALISMAN

We got to the Mexican border of *Talisman*. Gabriela and I got in line to pass through the border. There was not a huge line as I was expected. At the border we handed the Mexican immigration the false Mexican birth certificates. There I was in front of two Mexican immigration officers, a woman and a man. They had my false birth certificate in hand. The birth certificate was from the state of Sonora. I knew enough about Mexico to answer all the questions they wish to ask. When I spoke, I did so in my natural accent without making an effort to change it. When they heard me speak, they handed over my birth certificate, welcomed me to Mexico, and allowed me through the gate. It was easy as that.

I laughed at the idea of doing the same thing at the U.S border, if it was only a matter of answering questions I have no doubt they too would have allow me through. Unfortunately, the United States make it a little bit more difficult than just answering questions.

From the other side of the bridge I was able to see

and hear immigration customs speak with Gabriela. It did not go quite as well for her. Gabriela was able to correctly answer every question. Although she did so, the immigration officer did not believe a word she said. He confiscated her birth certificate and did not allow her to pass through. The immigration officer accused Gabriela of being from Honduras. They wanted to know where she had gotten the birth certificate. They were trying to persuade her to say that she was paying me to smuggle her through Mexico with destination to the United States. When I saw that they were giving Gabriela a hard time, I crossed the bridge back to Guatemala. Immigration customs told me that they were not going to allow Gabriela to enter Mexico because she was from Honduras. So I stayed in Guatemala along with her. I had to find a different route.

I was going to cross her to Mexico one way or another even if we had to climb a wall or swim a river. At first I imagined an obstacle of that sort; but no, it's nothing like that, there are no walls, there's no swimming, and there are no Mexican border patrol units to run away from. It's nothing as I had imagined. As we got closer to the border we saw that there was none of that. What we saw was a river, waist deep, and many wooden rafts. People were coming and going on those rafts. I asked a man how much the fee to get across was. The fee was ten Guatemalan quetzals for each person. We paid the fee, hopped onto one of the rafts and off we were heading to Mexico.

We crossed in bright day light. There was nothing covert about crossing the border. Immigration officers were actually watching the rafts haul Central American immigrants into their territory and did nothing to stop it. It almost seem like they wanted us to make it across. I was baffled by their idly reaction and I wonder why were they allowing this.

The first city entering into Mexico from Guatemala is

the city of *Hidalgo* in the state of Chiapas. The city of Hidalgo is not a safe place to be in. Central Americans make it unsafe. The city of Hidalgo is flooded with Central Americans immigrants with the dream of heading to the United States. Within the crowd of immigrants that enter Mexico there are also fugitives from the Mara Salvatrucha or (MS13); killers and rapists. Thereafter our arrival to the city of Hidalgo, we took a taxi to the city of *Tapachula* which is about twenty five minutes away. We settled at a hotel always looking for the most comfortable prices. We took the rest of the day to rest. My goal was to get to the state of Sonora where I know people willing to help me.

Chiapas is the state with the most immigration checkpoints in all of Mexico making it the most difficult state to go through. Getting Gabriela out of Chiapas was going to be a huge task. She knew that she was not capable of fooling immigration officers to make them think she was Mexican.

Above all, I could not afford to send her back to El Salvador. If I continued the trip with her, I was placing myself at risk of getting charge for smuggling an undocumented person across Mexico. That meant years of jail time for me. It was too much at stake, a hand that I was not going to gamble with, or attempt to bluff my way out. We decided that she was going to stay in Tapachula. I was going to travel to Sonora on my own. In Sonora I knew the right people that were able to get me a false marriage certificate. With that in hand, Gabriela was able to travel through Mexico without any issues.

I bought the bus ticket to Sonora. I still had my false Mexican birth certificate. I had gone through the most difficult immigration checkpoints without issues. We came to a checkpoint right before entering the state of Oaxaca. My luck came to an end when I encountered an officer in-charge that was apparently having a bad day, a brute female that went by the book. She told me she did not care if I was Mexican. I was going to be detained because I could not provide picture identification. The rest of the immigration officers wanted to let me go, but she was the boss. They never doubted that I was Mexican not for a moment. They kept going through my bag searching for drugs or weapons that I might have been carrying. Sonora has a bad reputation for trafficking drugs and weapons. An officer ran the name on the birth certificate, but there was no such person in the system, it was a made-up name which only made things worse.

They were beginning to think I was a fugitive; maybe not a fugitive, but definitely that I was hiding something. They placed me in a holding cell and told me they were going to turn me in to the custody of federal officials for further investigation. From the window of the holding cell I was able to see the officer had the birth certificate in her hand and was making the call to federal authorities. I banged the door and gestured an officer to come over. I told him the truth, which I was born in El Salvador and gave him my real name. At first he thought I was taking him for a ride. He did not believe me until I shown him my Salvadoran I.D.

In the morning I was taken to a transit immigration facility located in Tapachula where they process all the deportations. They had the intentions of deporting me to El Salvador. They never imagined that I had the intentions to buck on them.

CHAPTER 20
IMMIGRATION INSTITUTION AND ITS CORRUPTION

The *Instituto Nacional de Migracion* or (INM) in Tapachula is a transit institution, where all immigrants are taken to be process for deportation.

I've been in various institutions, detentions, prisons, and facilities throughout my life. The INM in Tapachula was obvious to me that it was built exclusively for transit purposes and for housing. It was not meant to hold immigrants for long periods of time. The INM has many holding cells without bunk beds. Mattresses are handed out to some of the immigrants. For, there are not enough mattresses for everyone. The rest are issued unwashed, filthy blankets to sleep on.

Immigrants from Central America are deported almost nightly by bus. They are only held there one or two days before they are deported. Immigrants from other countries such as Brazil or Colombia are held there two or three months while they wait for their plane tickets.

In spite of the INM being a transit facility it's also use to illegal house immigrants under its exasperating conditions. The institution houses immigrants who are mentally ill and physically impaired. It also houses refugees from Central America, Cuba, Africa, Nepal, Haiti, and Bangladesh amongst many other countries. Immigrants awaiting deportation do not realize the conditions of the institution because they are only passing through. However, the refugee immigrants that cannot return to their country suffer from duress of stress.

The institution does not provide the standard orange jumpsuits that are used in holding facilities. The institution does not provide nail or hair clippers, combs or razors. In a matter of weeks refugees have a grotesque appearance with long hair, long beard, and long fingernails.

Furthermore, the institution does not allow writing material like paper and pen, it does not count with televisions, does not count with board games like chess, checkers, or a deck of cards; it does not even count with a basketball or soccer ball although the institution has the courts. In short, the institution is not appropriate for housing purposes.

I spoke with refugees from different countries. They all had a heartbreaking story to tell. Nevertheless, not all refugees had a heartbreaking story. I met two Americans that were requesting for refuge: One was from Arkansas and the other from Florida. They did not want to return to the United States. They could not get a story straight as to why they did not want to go back to the United States. That made me wonder about them and I kept my distance from both of them. They both gave me bad vibes.

I also met a Mexican guy from *Nuevo Leon*. His name is Marcos. We got along well. I spent most of my time exercising and conversing with Marcos. He too had spent many years in a federal prison for illegal reentry. Marcos told me he was fed up living in Mexico. He was there because he was claiming to be from Nicaragua. He was looking for a free trip to Nicaragua. He wanted to meet up with his girlfriend he had there. Marcos said he had manage to fool them once before. But this time the Nicaraguan consulate was not buying his story. He was giving Marcos a hard time with the deportation. Marcos had spent months in Nicaragua until him and his girlfriend got into a fight and he left back to Mexico. He knew his way around Nicaragua real well, and he spoke like one of them when he felt like it. That only goes to show that no one is completely happy with where they at, or where there born, we're only happy with where we think we are heading.

The holding cells in which we were locked away were like ovens and lacked proper ventilation. There was constant smoking of cigarettes and cannabis in which the officers sold. Due to the lack of mattresses, every night people fought over them. Some immigrants tried to share the mattress by sleeping in two, others slept sitting down on the bench. The nights were restless because of the warm temperature and the constant noise. Still no one complained about the conditions because they would only be there a day or two before getting deported.

We were locked away with our fellow countrymen. Salvadorans in one holding cell, Hondurans in another, Guatemalans in another and so forth. Both Africans and Arabs were placed in a holding cell of their own. Housing was done this way making it easier to load up the buses during the deportation process. At four in the afternoon, the Guatemalan cell was open and names would be call out for deportation. At eleven at night Honduras was process and the Salvadorans were processed at one in the morning. Unfortunately for me, I happened to be in one of the loudest holding cells. The Salvadoran and Honduran holding cells were the loudest and the most troublesome.

They would mock the officers calling them "*smurfs*" instead of officers because of their blue uniform. They would bang the doors, sang songs, and made strange noises all night until they were call for deportation. They were eager to arrive in their country so that they may hit a U-turn and come right back to Mexico with the dream of arriving to the United States. There are many that have spent years chasing this dream. The obsession of one day making it to the United States has created a psychological disorder, I call the *railroad syndrome*. I call it that because they spend years living by the railroad tracks ridding the train which is best known as the "*bestia*" or the "beast."

I could see that it was not going to be an easy fight, but it was going to be worth it. First thing was first; I needed to find a way out of that holding cell.

Upon my arrival to the INM, I had noticed some single cells that had their own beds and restrooms inside. They were empty. I asked a refugee from Senegal that spoke six or seven different languages, what those cells were for. The cells were there for people with chronic illness or handicaps. There are a lot of immigrants that passes through the INM that have lost a leg or an arm while riding on top of the train. The train is the most common, inexpensive, and fastest way to travel through Mexico, but also the most dangerous. This is why the Central Americans have named this train, the "beast."

They call it that for a bad reason. To ride the beast means to wrestle with this monster for three or four days with little sleep and little food open to the perils that come their way. Three or four days are what take to get to the United States border ridding the beast. Hundreds travel on top of the beast every day. Very few make it to the United States border. Most are captured by Mexican immigration, some are thrown off the beast or fall from the beast during the pandemonium of immigration pursuits. Losing an arm or a leg is not the worst thing that could happen to an immigrant when they are thrown from the beast. Young girls are who suffer the most. They become victims of gang rape by the Mara Salvatrucha who are assigned to patrol the beast.

Impaired and chronic-ill immigrants did not like to be in the single cells by themselves. They preferred to be with everyone else, amidst the madness. I got the idea of pretending to be asthmatic. I told an officer about my alleged chronic illness. I said; *"Mr. Officer I suffer from asthma and the cigarette smoke is affecting me."* He did not seem to take me seriously or simply did not care.

I used an old trick from prison that's use to get medical attention a.s.a.p. The trick is called the "fish." All you have to do is pretend you a fish out of water and flop around. At night I told the Salvadorans in the cell to bang the door as loud as they could to get the attention of an officer. They were more than willingly to make all the noise that they could. They yelled at the top of their lungs that a man was dying. When the officers came to the cell I was in the ground pretending an asthma attack. They rush me out in a stretcher to a nurse where they provided me with an inhaler, which I later sold for fifty pesos. The act I had put up was worth it because I was able to get the cell that I wanted.

Finally I had peace of mind in my new cell. What I needed next was pen and paper, and legal material pertinent to immigration law and the Mexican Constitution. I was positive that we, refugees were being illegally housed there. Upon my request for asylum to the Refugee Committee I was provided with a legal document in which stated all of my rights I had as an asylum applicant. I analyzed the document. The rights that were stipulated on the document conflicted with our housing conditions. Most of the refugees were not able to understand these rights because everything was written in Spanish, or did not know how to interpret the law. Nonetheless, the document was cleared to me.

The best way to manifest any kind of violation in an institution is by a hunger strike. Any convict knows this.

It's most effective when many people participate in it. For this I needed to unite all refugees. Only this was going to be a task within itself. Everyone in the INM was too divided, Africans and Central Americans were always disputing with one another. They would argue over the chow hall line. They fought over mattresses and blankets. No one used the words; excuse me, pardon, or I'm sorry. They all behaved like children whining to the officers every minute of the day.

The first Spanish words Africans learned how to say were; *"El Salvador mucho problema,"* or *"Honduras mucho problema."* No one complained about the Guatemalans, they were the most pacific of all. I expressed to my fellow immigrants what I intended to do, and why. They did not seem interested on joining a hunger strike. The truth is that they lacked the willpower to go without food. They were always famishing. Each time the officers called out *"chow time!"* chaos broke out with everyone running pushing each other around. The officers tried to keep an order by one day calling the Africans first and Central Americans second. The following day Central Americans ate first and the Africans ate second. The Afro-Hondurans would get in line with the Africans and the Central Americans and would eat twice until the officers discovered their scam.

Meanwhile, I had found a way to make money. I was making a lot of profit by exchanging currency. I bought American dollars from the Salvadorans upon their arrival for twelve pesos per dollar, and resold them to the Salvadorans prior to their departure at eighteen Mexican pesos per dollar. I also bought the Guatemalan quetzals at one per one, and resold it at two Mexican pesos per one quetzal. I used some of the money to bribe an officer.

First, the officer brought me writing material. The following week he brought me a cellphone with a micro

SD card I had requested. The cellphone gave me access to the internet and calls. That's how I was able to inform Gabriela that I was back in Tapachula locked away in the INM. I told her that I had requested for asylum and was going to remain there for three months to six months. That's what I had been told. She was devastated by the news.

I used the internet on the cellphone to download the Mexican Constitution and immigration articles based on refugees. I wrote petitions for human rights and the refugee commission. The cellphone was also use to take pictures of the conditions in which we were living. I saved the pictures on the micro SD memory card. I went on the hunger strike thereafter. The INM officers were not bothered the first two days. The third day they tried to get me to eat. My petition to them was clear cut; I wanted to speak with human rights. If I was going to be house there for three to six months, I at least wanted fundamental privileges; access to haircuts, nail clippers, board games, and writing material.

The INM did not want me to speak with human rights, they were avoiding it. Each time I requested to speak with human rights an immigration officer would say, *"Just go back to El Salvador, come back and request for asylum from the outside."* Otherwise, he said, *"you'll remain in the institution."* The advice to return to a country where my life was at risk did not make any sense. And I expressed that to him. The INM discourages refugees from applying for asylum. They try to sway them to signing their deportation. They do it all the time.

The immigration officer in-charge of the INM had the kitchen prepared special plates which were sent to my cell. The food looked very tempting but I remained abstinent. At one point they had sent me some tuna sandwiches which I like very much, but I declined it as well. After a week of not eating, the lack of food began to show. I had lost a lot of weight and I felt weak. Fruit and bread was brought to me by Marcos and some of the refugees. Nonetheless, I refused their offers. I wanted the hunger strike to physically show on me. They were going to have to take me out in a stretcher before I took a single bite of food. I told Marcos and the refugees that brought me food. After ten days of hunger strike, the INM became worried and had no choice but to call human rights.

A representative of human rights by the name of Mr. Sanchez came to my cell. The impression of his face told me I did not look good. I told him all the concerns I had; the lack of privileges, housing conditions, and more importantly, the illegal refugee housing. I emphasized a clause that was on the document which stated that every asylum applicant had the right to *freely* come and go anywhere within the state of Chiapas, outside of Chiapas this right was null and only then were we expose to be detained. I told him that it was illogical to have immunity and be detained at the same time. I handed him my petitions written based immigration law and the Constitution of Mexico. He asked how I was able to obtain all of that information. I bluntly told him I had a cellphone in which I had also used to take pictures of the institution.

Moreover, the Cubans had made videos that were sent to a Cuban reporter in Miami narrating what they were going through. And just to let him know that I was not bluffing, I handed him the micro SD card the officer had brought me. All of the pictures I had taken were on that micro SD card. I made it clear to him that those pictures were also going to go public if nothing was done.

The condition of the INM was causing many of the refugees to revoke their request for asylum. I reminded Mr. Sanchez of the incident that occurred on May 10th of 2016 (Mexican mother's day). On that afternoon a refugee from El Salvador climbed the basketball pole, he stood on top of the hoop, some of the Central Americans brought out mattresses to place below as they attempted to convince him to come down. The Salvadorans that shared the holding cell with him knew that he was a troubled man. He had asked the Salvadorans in the cell to take pity on him and choke him to death. This man was not playing when he asked to be killed.

The guards were informed what was happening; they had all the time in the world to act upon the matter. Instead they laugh about it saying that he was not going to jump. Some guards were willing to bet on it. They even ordered the immigrants to remove the mattresses and take them back inside, which they complied. After all the mattresses were removed the distressful man took a look at the sky as he mumbled some words, waived at the sky and took a leap forward, head down first.

Throughout the fall he kept his hands behind his back. This is something not easily forgotten; the sound of his skull hitting the concrete ground and the sight thereafter. Seconds before it happened there was laughter and officers joking about it. Then all of sudden, everyone was quite, and the people appeared to have been frozen in time. The guards did not know how to respond.

On the other side of the court, a native from Honduras ran, climbed the basketball pole with the intention to do the same thing. For, he was another refugee. The Africans were the only ones quick to react and ran after him. Other Africans crowded beneath the basketball hoop ready to catch him. They managed to bring him down. Not the guards, not the Central Americans, not the Arabs, no one responded with the swiftness that the Africans did. In spite of the cultures, of the differences, and conflicts that existed between the two, the instinct of humanity took control of the situation. My hat went off to the Africans that day for saving that man's life.

The Mexican commission for refugees, and human

rights were told a different version. Mr. Sanchez promised that he was going to help me. He had found our conversation intriguing. As I was finishing up with Mr. Sanchez, tumult broke out in the institution. The Cubans had already told me what they were going to do when human rights came. They were frustrated of being in there already and they wanted to demonstrate their frustration to human rights by igniting mattresses; there was smoke and fire everywhere and then there was water everywhere as the officers used the fire host to put out the fire.

The Hondurans and Africans used that distraction to force themselves in the kitchen and ate all the food that was going to be used to feed the institution. The rest of the immigrants went without dinner that night. Mr. Sanchez ran out the place. I was feeling very feeble from the hunger strike, but I could not resist from breaking out in laughter as I was witnessing what was happening around me.

Amazingly the next day the Cubans were released. They should not have been there in the first place. They were there because INM officials were looking to get some money out of them to allow them to continue their trip to the United States. An immigration officer had offered me already to amend my immigration for two-thousand dollars. I did not have that money otherwise I'd have taken the offer at that time.

That day I ended the hunger strike knowing that the INM was not happy at all with the things I was doing and that gave me pleasure. An immigration officer had provided me with the instruments that made that possible, but he did not care as long as I kept bribing him. It was through this same immigration officer that I found out why the INM encourages refugees to sign their deportations.

There are two hundred reasons why they wanted me to return to El Salvador. The United States rewards the INM two-hundred dollars for each immigrant that's deported. There's lucrative in the flow of immigrants in Mexico. It all made sense to me why the INM observed so idly as Central American immigrants crossed the river. An immigrant in Guatemalan soil is worthless, but in Mexican soil he is worth two-hundred dollars. I'm almost certain that the rafts that are used to transport immigrants across the river are obliged to pay a fee to the INM in order to keep operating. The INM have certainly found a way to scam the United States government.

I do not know the capacity of the buses that are used to transport immigrants, but they are huge. Almost nightly they ship anywhere from twelve to twenty buses back to Central America. The United States has also gone as far as donating equipment of latest technology for example; infra-red detectors and Gama rays to assist the INM in Chiapas catch Central American immigrants. This technology along with the two-hundred dollar incentive makes Chiapas the most difficult state of Mexico to cross through.

I became more convince in the United States' role when I saw them with my own eyes visiting the institution. I followed behind them as they walk inspecting the institution. They spoke English. They went into the kitchen to take a look of the food we ate. Of course that day we were serve a special dish. They looked inside the shower area. It could have not been more evident that the institution is financed by the United States, undoubtedly tax dollars. I approached the group and I asked, in English of course, if they were aware that they were housing asylum applicants there.

They asked my nationality, I told them I was born in El Salvador. None of the Mexican officials knew what I was saying. They asked me how long I had been there. By then I had been there for more than two months. I had long beard, long hair and long nails; I looked grotesque! When they heard this, they turned to look at one another, I was able to tell that they did not like what they were hearing, and the immigration officers also were quick to notice their displeasure. They asked if there more asylum applicants, which of course there was: hundreds of them.

I found out later, that the institution responsible to house asylum applicants is located in Mexico City. That's where all refugees should have been house. Nevertheless, it cost money to transport refugees there, money that the INM did not want to spend.

A few days later an immigration officer came to my cell at night. Everyone was under lock key by then. He told me to quietly pack up all my belongings they were going to release me. They did not want me to say a word to the rest of the immigrants that I was living. I did not like the idea of being release at ten o'clock at night and being told not to say a word. I knew that the INM were upset at the things that I had done, there was no telling what they were planning to do with me. But I complied. I gathered all my belongings, disobeyed the officer by telling my Mexican friend Marcos that I was leaving. I wished him the best of luck on his task of getting to Nicaragua.

I had tried my best to do things in unity with the rest of the refugees, Black and Brown color did not matter to me. I succumbed to doing everything on my own. I had stood my ground all by myself, now I was being rewarded for doing so. I was detained on March 9th of 2016, and released May 16th of 2016. I was release for "humanitarian reasons" they told me. It really did not matter to me what was the reason for my release. What matters is that my effort to do the right thing paid off. The bottom line is that Mexico deemed me the second opportunity I've sought for so many years, and in so many countries. And for that my friends I'm grateful.

MY UPHILL BATTLE

CHAPTER 21
IN THE QUEST FOR CUJO

Upon my release from the institution, I took a taxi to the room where I had left Gabriela prior to heading to Sonora. I still had the cellphone I bought from the immigration officer with me, but I did not bother to call her. I wanted to surprise her. It was dark already when I knocked at the door. At first she did not want to open, she opened when she heard my voice. It took her a few seconds to recognize me. I still look like a caveman with long hair and with a long beard. Her eyes tear up before she made a smile.

Getting detained by the INM had worked out for the best. If I'd have made it to Sonora, I'd have to live under a false identity perhaps risking jail time and deportation. In the middle of June of 2016 I received yet more good news. I was told by the commission for refugees that they had found ample reason to believe that my life in El Salvador was in danger. Amnesty International provided information that attested my persecution claim. Thus, I was bequeathed permanent residency in Mexico never again do I have to worry about being return to El Salvador. That was the happiest day of my life. I felt as though I had won the lottery. Nonetheless, there were still a few things missing to complete my happiness. Gabriela needed to legalize her immigration status, and I needed to bring Cujo to Mexico.

Going back to El Salvador for Cujo was my next hurdle coming up. It was a nearly impossible one. I had vowed that I was going to return for Cujo and that's what I intend to do. I contacted Cesar and he told me Cujo was ill. He was not eating anymore, he looked as though he was dying, and all he did all day was sniffing the air. Cujo was sad. He had waited almost three months for me to go back for him. I explained to him that I was going to return. I did not know exactly when, but by all means I was going return for him.

More of my long time homeboys had contacted me by then to see how things were with me. The timing could not have been better. I was going to need some help for the trip to El Salvador. I spoke with *Chayo*. *Chayo* is *Lonely's* youngster brother. The last time I saw *Chayo* he was only eleven-years old. That was more than twenty-five years ago. I used to stay over at his house when I was just a teen. His house was my second home.

Another person I heard from was *Gus*. I've known *Gus* for more than two decades, and I never knew until recently that he was born in Nicaragua. *Gus* has always been kind-hearted and he is one of the most loyal persons I've ever met. With him, I learned how to jug a *40oz. Old English* when I was only twelve-years old. We were drinking partners from an early age. I was indeed very happy to have heard from these two old friends. *Chayo*, like *Bad Boy*, has also turned his life around and has become Christian. *Gus* and *Chayo* told me the same thing *Bad Boy* had told me; *"God has a will for you…"* and I was actually starting to belief that. I was beginning to see a revelation in my life, a path of prosperity.

I told *Gus* and *Chayo* I was heading back to El Salvador. I told them the reason, and added that Cujo was not just any old dog to me. *Gus* was able to empathize. For, he too has a dog that's very dear to him, a bluenose pit-bull by the name of *Blue*. Whatever the reason was my friends, my brothers, were always more than willing to help me. *Gus* and *Chayo* financed the trip to El Salvador. All they asked in return was for me to take care of myself.

Gabriela did not like the idea of returning to El Salvador, she tried to talk me out of it saying that we were not going to be able get Cujo to Mexico. Her pleads were of no use. Gabriela has always been frightened to do things unofficially, with me she had to learn how to bend the rules. She feared something could have gone wrong, but at the end she does not stay behind no matter how scare she is, and follows me to face any obstacle that stands along my away. We took the trip in late June of 2016. Cujo was eight hours away (292 miles).

Gabriela kept asking throughout the way: "How are we going to get Cujo across the borders?" How are we going to transport him through Guatemala?" "What if we get caught?" She was worried about going to jail for transporting an undocumented canine for Christ sake! She was becoming annoying. I explained to her that the only way people went to jail for transporting animals was when they were wild animals, such as tigers, or monkeys and not domestic animals. She was still doubtful.

Her head was filled with worries. She had every reason to worry. The truth was I was worried too. I did not know how I was going to transport Cujo to Mexico. When we arrived to the Salvadoran border we enter the country through a blind spot avoiding registration at the check point. We had left from Mexico at five in the morning and arrived in El Salvador at about two in the afternoon. Cesar was already waiting for us when we arrived at his house.

Cujo was extremely weak but that did not stop him from running toward me, he would not stop wagging his tail and would not stop barking at me as if he was complaining why I had took so long to come get him. I fed him, and he ate in abundance. He followed me everywhere I went; to the restroom, to the kitchen, and outside the house. Cesar had tried his best to care for him, he really did. Nevertheless, Cujo had been stricken by poignant and there was nothing Cesar could have done to make that go away.

We spent the night at Cesar's house with plans to leave in the morning. The following morning I said my farewell to my friend Cesar and thank him for taking care of Cujo while I was gone. There were no issues taking Cujo to the Guatemalan border. El Salvador allows dogs on board as long as they wear a muzzle. Twenty minutes later we were at the Guatemalan border. Once again we circumvented the check point by going through the same back door channel we had entered. We were not the only group taking that channel that day. There was a group of six Mara Salvatrucha members heading to Guatemalan, possibly even heading to Mexico. Gabriela as usual got scared when she saw them. I could tell because she always squeezes my arm when she is frightened by something or someone.

We walked a few feet behind the group. I whispered to Gabriela to try her best not to demonstrate her fear. The group kept turning back, to look at Cujo. They asked where we were heading. I responded. Another asked if Cujo was mean, I said "*yes*," and warned him not to get too close to him. I had removed the muzzle when we got off the bus, and I was glad to have done so. It was a fifteen-minute walk through a lonely dirt road. If Cujo would have not been with us perhaps there would have been a different story.

Once we got to the other side of the border we

headed to the terminal, which was at walking distance. There were no direct buses to *Tecun Uman* (Mexican border). Those buses had to be taken in Guatemala City. Son first thing we had to do was take a bus to the capital. From Guatemala City we had to catch the bus to Tecun Uman. The other problem we encounter was that the bus to Guatemala City only left at four o'clock in the morning. I already knew about their no-pets policy. Still, I bought the bus tickets for four o'clock in the morning not giving a dam about their policy. Gabriela was pessimistic as always, and repeated the same questions she had been asking throughout the way. I did not even try to explain to her, I just gave her *that* look.

I was going to worry about getting Cujo aboard at its adequate time. Meanwhile we needed to worry where we were going to spend the night. We found a room, but dogs were not allowed inside the rooms. I tried my best to convince the lady in-charge to allow him in. I even offered to pay extra. Although she did not allow Cujo in the room, she allowed him to stay in the patio. It was good enough for me and I paid for the night.

When we left to the room, Cujo begin to bark with that loud bark he has, and he would not stop until he saw me again. It was raining that night as always in Central America. We did not bother to bring extra clothes. It was going to be an in-and-out objective. I sat next to Cujo and petted him while we got soaking wet. When he finally went to sleep I went back into the room. A few minutes later he went at it again. This time Gabriela went out to keep him company. For a second we thought Cujo was going to have us kicked out the place due to the ruckus he was causing. We went back and forth a couple of times, at the end all three of us slept in the patio under the rain.

We got to the terminal before four o'clock to look for the bus driver. When I found him I spoke with him and told him that I was going to bring a dog along. At first he tried to explain the company's policy about pets. I offered him to pay him two-hundred quetzals if he allowed the dog on the bus. He agreed, as long as I took responsibility of cleaning after Cujo. I was okay with that. Cujo likes to have privacy during his moment with nature. The bus driver asked me to take the last sit on the bus. It was going to be a two-hour drive to the City of Guatemala. We arrived after seven in the morning.

The bus to Tecun Uman was scheduled for the next hour. We purchased the tickets, again knowing that no pets were allowed aboard. And once again I decided to approach the bus driver in an attempt to bribe him to allow Cujo on the bus. He did not yield. I offered him twice as much than the last bus driver but he refused to take it. He was being arrogant. His arrogance was making me upset, and he was enjoying the moment because he had a smirk on his face that I wanted to slap. I had not slept much the night before, my clothes were still soaked, and yet there I was trying to be Mr. Nice Guy. I was left with no other choice but to use the Mara Salvatrucha scare tactic. I lifted my shirt exposing the tattoos on my body, nowhere did it indicated I was a member of the Mara Salvatrucha, but his eyes bulged out scare out of his wits as he thought I was a member.

I made the meanest face I was able to do and told him that Cujo was getting on board, or otherwise. It worked! The bus driver allowed Cujo on board without further issues. I did not even have to pay him extra. I did not like the fact that I had to strong-arm Cujo's way in the bus, but that was the only thing that came to my mind at the moment. It was another five hours to get to the Mexican border. We arrived at to Tecun Uman at about three o'clock in the afternoon.

The river is only waist deep, but we took the raft to avoid getting wet. Our clothes were already dry from the night before. Half way through the river, Cujo leaped into the water pulling me by the leash along with him. I fell into the water. Gabriela could not stop laughing, neither did the people on the raft, and so did I; after all, I finally had Cujo with me. There was good reason to be happy. We had managed to bring Cujo to Mexico with less than one-hundred dollars. The biggest hurdle was left behind.

When we got to Tapachula, I called Cesar to let him know we had made it safe. I mentioned to him what Cujo had done. He chuckled at the thought of Cujo pulling me along into the water. Cesar told me that he used to take Cujo fishing almost daily, which is how Cesar makes his living. Cujo had grown very fond of the water during the time that I was gone. I'd have never imagined that because he really hated the water.

CHAPTER 22
THE STRIFE HAS COME TO AN END

Cujo, Gabriela, and I are all together in Mexico safe and sound. All that was needed now was to legalize Gabriela's immigration status. The only way to do that was through marriage.

In spite of the hazards of our journey Gabriela never thought of leaving my side not for a single minute. We had faced all obstacles together. What else proof did I needed to show me that Gabriela loves me unconditionally? Marrying her would not be a mistake that I will later regret. On January 17th of 2017 Gabriela and I tied the knot.

When we arrived back from El Salvador with Cujo I heard of yet more of longtime friends. I heard from Blanca Morales my old Jr. High school friend. I also heard from my homegirl Nubia Flores (*Beaver*), her mother Doña Rogelia still remembered me. To me it seemed like every time I needed to accomplish a goal, an angel was sent to me. My goal at that time was to marry Gabriela. This goal would not have been possible without the help of these two angels. They made it happened. At our wedding there were no guests, there was no celebration, no wedding cake or rings nothing of that sort. We have postponed all that for the meantime. There will be time for it later.

Throughout my uphill trek I realized where nowhere is, and where nowhere leads to; who are my friends and are not. One should never be afraid to head towards the direction of nowhere. It may lead you to your myriad success. It led me to a country where I can freely come and go as I please without the worry of being killed for no reason, and where at night you can still hear giggling children play out on the streets. In El Salvador these things are unheard off for someone like me.

Though above all, I'm legal in the country that best suits me; I'm married to a woman that loves me; and lastly, I have been honored with the opportunity to become a father. None of these things was I able to gain in the six years that I lived in El Salvador. The revelation is self-evident now.

My homeboy *Bad Boy*, *Gus*, and *Chayo* were right after all, God has a will for me; for all of us in fact. A will that had to be fulfilled by an uphill struggle, and through struggle alone! The uphill road has come to an end for me, and from its peak I can see the downhill side of it and let me tell you, it's laid out with wonderful splendors up ahead.

MY UPHILL STRUGGLE

My knees tremble they feel weak,

My feet are moist from the puddles I've walked upon,

From the distance that I've ran.

The arms are tired

From the heavy load that I carried

On my shoulders it is bury.

The stomach aches from lack of food that is not receiving,

The eyes get tired from the sleep yet not given.

Though, I will not stop., must continue forward,

The sun shines in the other side of the hill,

And I'm almost there to accomplish

--God's giving will.

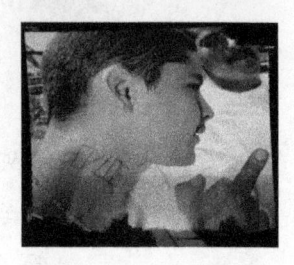

(Above) 111st and Vermont, Los Angeles. The place that was known as the hood.

(Below right) Me at the age of 13-years old with Cheecho on the background.

MY UPHILL BATTLE

Corcoran SHU-yard 75ft. by 25ft. where the fights took place.

SHU inmates in their cells.

SHU inmates in combat.

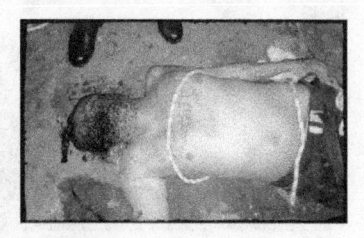

Before and after pictures of dead Salvadoran gang members. Taken by and posted by the *Sombra Negra*.

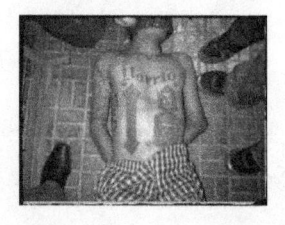

Pictures of Gabriela and me in the island of Petén Las Flores Guatemala.

(Bottom right) My best friend Cujo.

The river that divides Guatemala and Mexico. Rafts that are used to transport Central American immigrants across the river.

The train that's best known as The Beast. Hundreds of immigrants travel on it risking their lives chasing the American dream.

MY UPHILL BATTLE

(Above) My room and kitchen in Chiapas Mexico.

(Below left) Gabriela with an ill-stricken Cujo in El Salvador the time when we went to pick him up.

(Below right) Gabriela with Cujo in Chiapas Mexico upon our arrival to Mexico.

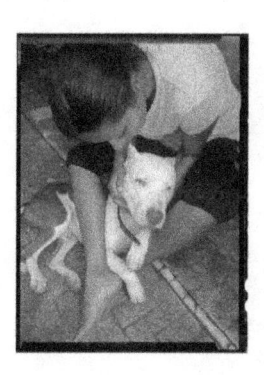

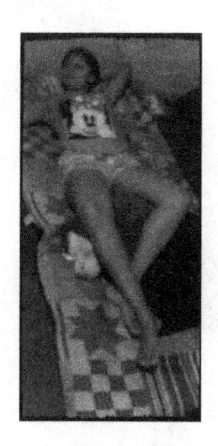

My homeboy Chayo, Lonely, Rascal, Cricket, Bad Boy.

My homeboy Yankee with his daughters.

My homeboy Gus with his beer.

ABOUT THE AUTHOR

Marvin was born in El Salvador in 1976. He grew up in Los Angeles California. He spent a total of 17 years behind bars. Now lives in Mexico with his wife Gabriela and his dog Cujo. He spends most of his time with both of them enjoying every single moment of his life.

www.ingramcontent.com/pod-product-compliance
Lightning Source LLC
LaVergne TN
LVHW092140230425
809465LV00024B/149